AN APPROACH TO CYBERNETICS

£1.00

An approach to Cybernetics

Gordon Pask

WITH A PREFACE BY WARREN S. McCULLOCH

MASSACHUSETTS INSTITUTE OF TECHNOLOGY

A RADIUS BOOK / HUTCHINSON

HUTCHINSON & CO (*Publishers*) LTD
3 Fitzroy Square, London W1

London Melbourne Sydney Auckland
Wellington Johannesburg Cape Town
and agencies throughout the world

First published 1961
This edition March 1968
Second impression October 1968
Third impression July 1972

To Elizabeth

Printed in Great Britain by litho on smooth wove paper
by Anchor Press, and bound by Wm. Brendon,
both of Tiptree, Essex

ISBN 0 09 086810 2 (cased)
0 09 086811 0 (paper)

Contents

CONTENTS

Preface

THIS book is not for the engineer content with hardware, nor for the biologist uneasy outside his specialty; for it depicts that miscegenation of Art and Science which begets inanimate objects that behave like living systems. They regulate themselves and survive: They adapt and they compute: They invent. They co-operate and they compete. Naturally they evolve rapidly.

Pure mathematics, being mere tautology, and pure physics, being mere fact, could not have engendered them; for creatures to live, must sense the useful and the good; and engines to run must have energy available as work: and both, to endure, must regulate themselves. So it is to Thermodynamics and to its brother $\Sigma p \log p$, called Information Theory, that we look for the distinctions between work and energy and between signal and noise.

For like cause we look to reflexology and its brother feedback, christened Multiple Closed Loop Servo Theory, for mechanical explanation of Entelechy in Homeostasis and in appetition. This is that governance, whether in living creatures and their societies or in our lively artifacts, that is now called Cybernetics.

But under that title Norbert Wiener necessarily subsumed the computation that, from afferent signals, forecasts successful conducts in a changing world.

To embody logic in proper hardware explains the laws of thought and consequently stems from psychology. For numbers the digital art is as old as the abacus, but it came alive only when Turing made the next operation of his machine hinge on the value of the operand, whence its ability to compute any computable number.

For Aristotelian logic, the followers of Ramon Lull, including Leibnitz, have frequently made machines for three, and sometimes four, classifications. The first of these to be lively computes contingent probabilities.

With this ability to make or select proper filters on its inputs,

9

such a device explains the central problem of experimental epistemology. The riddles of stimulus equivalence or of local circuit action in the brain remain only as parochial problems.

This is that expanding world of beings, man-made or begotten, concerning which Ross Ashby asked, 'How can such systems organize themselves?' His answer is, in one sense, too general and its embodiment, too special to satisfy him, his friends or his followers.

This book describes their present toil to put his ideas to work so as to come to grips with his question.

20th December, 1960.   WARREN S. McCULLOCH

1 The Background of Cybernetics

Introduction

CYBERNETICS is a young discipline which, like applied mathematics, cuts across the entrenched departments of natural science; the sky, the earth, the animals and the plants. Its interdisciplinary character emerges when it considers economy not as an economist, biology not as a biologist, engines not as an engineer. In each case its theme remains the same, namely, how systems regulate themselves, reproduce themselves, evolve and learn. Its high spot is the question of how they organize themselves.

A cybernetic laboratory has a varied worksheet – concept formation in organized groups, teaching machines, brain models, and chemical computers for use in a cybernetic factory. As pure scientists we are concerned with brain-like artifacts, with evolution, growth and development; with the process of thinking and getting to know about the world. Wearing the hat of applied science, we aim to create what Boulanger,[1] in his presidential address to the International Association of Cybernetics, called the instruments of a new industrial revolution – control mechanisms that lay their own plans.

The crux of organization is stability, for 'that which is stable' can be described; either as the organization itself, or some characteristic which the organization preserves intact. 'That which is stable' may be a dog, a population, an aeroplane, Jim Jones, Jim Jones's body temperature, the speed of a ship, or indeed, a host of other things.

In chemistry, for example, Le Chatellier's Principle is a statement that the equilibrial concentration of reactants in a closed vessel is stable, for it asserts that the assembly will react so as to nullify thermal or chemical disturbances. But the equilibrium, which is always implied by the word stability, is rarely of this simple kind. Jim Jones is in dynamic equilibrium with his environment. He is not energetically isolated and his constituent material is being continually built up and broken down and

11

interchanged. When we say 'Jim Jones is stable', we mean the form, the organization that we recognize as Jim Jones, is invariant. Again, if Jim Jones drives his motor car his behaviour is (statistically speaking) stable, and (in the sense that a destination is reached and no collision occurs) Jim Jones and his automobile are in equilibrium with their world.

Origins of Cybernetics

A great deal of cybernetics is concerned with how stability is maintained with 'control mechanisms'. One of the first of these to be treated explicitly was Watt's invention of the governor (a theoretical analysis was offered by Maxwell in 1865). The device illustrates a principle called *negative feedback*. A signal, indicating the speed of a steam engine, is conveyed to a power amplifying device (in this case, a steam throttle) in such a way that when the engine accelerates the steam supply is reduced. Hence, the speed is kept stable. The signalling arrangement is independent of energetic considerations, and it is legitimate to envisage the governor as a device which feeds back *information* in order to effect speed control.

Physiological Sources

Perhaps the earliest cybernetic thinking comes within the compass of physiology, where the key notions of information feedback and control appear as the ideas of reflex and homeostasis. In 1817 Magendie defined a reflex as an activity produced by a disturbance of some part of the body which travelled (over the dorsal nerve roots) to the central nervous system, and was reflected (through the ventral nerve roots) to the point of origin where it modified, stopped or reversed the original disturbance. The basic idea of signalling and directed activity is apparent (the common misinterpretation of a reflex as a mere relay action should be avoided). The elaboration of this idea in the early part of the present century, and the experimental study of reflexes up to and beyond Pavlov, is well known.

Whereas reflexis preserves the organism against the flux of its environment, homeostasis counters the internally generated changes which are prone to disrupt the proper structure and disposition of parts in the organism. Homeostatic mechanisms maintain the *milieu internale* of Claude Bernard, the proper values of acidity, water balance and metabolites – a body temperature which the cells of the body can tolerate. The first comprehensive study was published by Cannon in 1932[2] and there is a vast amount of recent work (to cite a few representative papers; Stanford Goldman[3] treating blood sugar control as a feedback mechanism, T. H. Benzinger[4] for a discussion of the thermal regulator in the hypothalamus, and Magoun, Peterson, Lindsley, and McCulloch[5] for a study of feedback in postural tremor).

In much, though not all, physiological control the brain is chief controller, and in effecting control, chief recognizer, rationalizer and arbiter. Hence cybernetic thinking stems also from psychology and in turn makes comment. Studying the brain we meet a feature common to most cybernetic investigations – the assembly is so large that its details always, and its general outline sometimes, remain necessarily obscure. Here the mathematical models of our science are particularly valuable. One kind of model is a network of formal neurones (a formal neurone is a construct, depicting the least set of properties which a real neurone, a constituent active cell of the brain, could possibly possess). McCulloch, who pioneered this field has reached a number of conclusions. In particular he and Pitts showed some years ago [69, 70] that plausible networks of these formal neurones were automata capable of many gambits, such as learning, the elaboration of gestalten and the embodiment of universals. Hence, the corresponding modes of mentality are neither surprising nor adventitious when they appear in the far more elaborate real brain.

Finally there is the question of 'purpose'. All the homeostatic and reflexive mechanisms are goal-directed and self-regulating. There is no magic about this and, whilst we can discern the goal, no mystery either. But when, as often happens, a goal is sought by several interacting mechanisms, or several goals appear to be sought by one, we might apply the term 'purposive' to the resulting behaviour. There is no suggestion of a vital force (and though we rightly marvel at the organization, there is no need to introduce teleological concepts). In particular we are likely to find purposive behaviour in assemblies like brains, which are large and incompletely observed. But I do not wish to give the impression that the generation of purposive or any other behaviour is enlodged within a particular assembly. In cybernetics we are thinking of an organization. Citing McCulloch's 1946 lecture, 'Finality and Form' '... some re-entrant paths lie within the central nervous system, others pass through remote parts of the body and still others, leaving the body by effectors, returning by receptors, traverse the external world. The functions of the first are, at present, ill defined, the second constitute the majority of our reflexes, the last our appetites and purposes . . .' Their totality is the organism we study in cybernetics.

Other Sources

In zoology and in embryology there used to be a problem equivalent to the teleological dilemma of purposive behaviour. Here it took the name equifinality. Driesch, for example, was led to believe in a vital force, because the development of sea urchin embryos seemed to be pre-determined 'from outside' since they reached the same final form even though crassly mutilated. By the early 1920's biologists were thinking in terms of organization (there is a classic paper of Paul Weiss,[6] which bears this out) and it became obvious that in a wholly pedestrian manner the whole of an organization is more than the sum of its parts. The mystique behind equifinality (which lay there because, from a circumscribed point of view, the parts *should* add up to the whole) evaporated like the apparent magic of purposiveness. Von Bertalanffy's thinking in this direction exerted considerable influence, not only in biology but also in the social sciences, and he gave the name *system* to the organization which is recognized and studied (we speculate about the system which is the organization of a leopard and not about the leopard itself). Further, von Bertalanffy realized that when we look at systems (which cyberneticians always do) many apparently dissimilar assemblies and processes show features in common.[7] He called the search for unifying principles which relate different systems, General Systems Theory.

General Systems Theory found little acceptance in engineering and had little relation to the physiological developments until the mid-1940's. About then, engineers had to make computing and control devices elaborate enough to exhibit the troublesome kinds of purposiveness already familiar in biology. Also it was in the 1940's that Julian Bigelow, then Rosenblueth and Wiener realized the significance of the organizational viewpoint, and had the insight to wed together the developments we have discussed and the rigorous mathematics of communication engineering.

Definitions of Cybernetics

Thus, cybernetics was born. Since then it has been variously defined. At one extreme, there is the original definition, 'the *science* of control and communication in the animal and the machine,' advanced by Norbert Wiener[8] when he adopted the word* in 1948 in the book *Cybernetics* which is the first complete statement of the discipline (a paper[9] anticipates a part of the argument). At the other extreme is Louis Couffignal's[10] proposal, put forward as an expansion in 1956, 'La Cybernetique est l'art d'assurer l'efficacite de l'action.' The gap between *science* and *art* is filled by a continuum of interpretations. Thus, Stafford Beer[11] looks upon cybernetics as the science of proper control within any assembly that is treated as an organic whole. In industry, for example, this could be the science of management. Also he regards Operational Research, in its widest sense, as the principal experimental method of cybernetics, the science. Ross Ashby,[12] on the other hand, gives emphasis to abstracting a controllable system from the flux of a real world (for abstraction is a prerequisite of talk about control), and he is concerned with the entirely general synthetic operations which can be performed upon the abstract image. He points out that cybernetics is no more restricted to the control of observable assemblies and the abstract systems that correspond with them, than geometry is restricted to describing figures in the Euclidean space which models our environment.

For my own part,[13] I subscribe to both Ashby's and Beer's view, finding them compatible. Their definitions are both included by Wiener's global dictum.

The cybernetician has a well specified, though gigantic, field of interest. His object of study is a system, either constructed, or so abstracted from a physical assembly, that it exhibits interaction between the parts, whereby one controls another, unclouded by the physical character of the parts themselves. He manipulates and modifies his systems often using mathematical techniques, but, because in practical affairs cybernetics is most usefully

* The world 'Cybernetics' was first used by Ampère as the title of a sociological study. It is derived from the Greek word for steersman.

applied to a very large system, he may also build mechanical artifacts to model them. Simply because the particulars are irrelevant, he can legitimately examine such diverse assemblies as genes in a chromosome, the contents of books in a library (with respect to information storage), ideas in brains, government and computing machines (with respect to the learning process).

Common Misconceptions

It is easy to misinterpret the whole idea and conclude that cybernetics is a trivial or even meaningless pursuit. We have to answer the kind of criticism offered by Buck[14] – that anything whatever can be a system – according to most cybernetic definitions of the word. But I believe an answer can be given, providing we do not confuse the strict identity of principle between the workings of several assemblies, which the cybernetician tries to embody in his abstract system, with mere facile analogy. The confusion does occur when people over-simplify the supposed activities of a cybernetician, perhaps, for a popular account of them, by expressing these activities in terms of a single experiment.

Let us suppose, for example, that Mr X is building a cybernetic model of some region of the brain. Mr X is approached by Mr Y who asks his profession. 'Cybernetician,' says Mr X. 'Such nonsense,' says Y, 'I've never heard of it, but,' he adds, 'I can see you're making a model of the brain. Be sensible and tell me whether you are a psychologist, or an electronic engineer.' If Mr X insists that he is neither, but a cybernetician, Y will make some private reservations and humour the man, pressing Mr X to describe his activity 'as though he were a psychologist' or 'as though he were an electronic engineer', because he can 'understand that sort of language'. For Y is convinced that X is making some electrical imitation of the brain. But if the device *is* a cybernetic model, then it is almost certainly a *very* poor imitation. In consonance with Beer[8] I submit that the workings of a cybernetic model are identical with some feature in the workings of a brain which is relevant to the control within a brain. Most likely, this feature is *not* readily describable in terms of psychology *or* electronics. So, having missed the point, Y is apt to depart under the impression that X is bad at psychology and bad at electronics and a little demented.

It is easy to cite brain models which are merely imitations; most well-behaved robots, most of the tidy automata that imitate a naughts and crosses player, nearly all of the maze solving machines (though there are some, like Deutsch's Rat,[15] which are used explicitly to illustrate an organizational principle rather than to imitate a response). There are not so many cybernetic models to choose from, but one of them, made by Ashby[16] and called the Homeostat, admirably illustrates the distinction. It is made up of four interacting regulators and an independent switching mechanism which changes the interconnections between these elements until a stable arrangement is reached. It can (from the viewpoint of psychology and engineering respectively) be dubbed a 'brain-like analogue' and a 'device for solving differential equations', for it does, rather imperfectly, display a brain-like behaviour and it will, rather eccentrically, solve differential equations. Its imperfections as an equation solver (which it is not meant to be) are obvious from its construction and have met with a good deal of heavy-handed criticism. Its imperfections as a brain-like analogue (which, once again, it is not meant to be) occur because at the level of functional analogy the organization of a homeostat is not particularly brainlike. It is only when we come to the level intended in the cybernetic abstraction that the self-regulation in a homeostat is *identical* with the self-regulation in a brain, and with reference to this feature the homeostat *is a* cybernetic model of all brains.

Summary

To summarize, a cybernetician adopts, so far as possible, an attitude which lays emphasis upon those characteristics of a physical assembly which are common to each discipline and 'abstracts' them into his 'system'.

This is not a prudent methodology, for it runs the risk of seeming to be impertinent. It is justified in so far as it *does* lead to effective control procedures, efficient predictions, and acceptable unifying theories (and whilst this is true of *any* science, the sanctions are rightly enough weighted against a Jack of all trades). But the risk, on balance, is worth while, for the cybernetic approach *can* achieve generality and yield rigorous comments upon *organization*.

2 Learning, Observation and Prediction

OBSERVERS are men, animals, or machines able to learn about their environment and impelled to reduce their uncertainty about the events which occur in it, by dint of learning. In this chapter we shall examine human observers who, because we have an inside understanding of their observational process, belong to a special category. For the moment, we shall not bother with HOW an observer learns, but will concentrate upon WHAT he learns about, i.e. what becomes more certain.*

As observers *we expect* the environment to change and try to describe those features that remain unchanged with the passage of time. An unchanging form of events due to the activity within an assembly is called a *behaviour*. The behaviour of a steam engine is a recurrent cycle of steam injection and piston movements that remains invariant. The behaviour of a cat is made up of performances like eating and sleeping and, once again, it is an invariant form selected from the multitude of things a cat might possibly do. The behaviour of a statue is a special case, for the statue is immobile, or to use an equivalent formalism, it changes at each instant of time into itself. We shall neglect the special case entirely. An 'assembly' is the dynamic part of an observer's environment, a piece of the real world, which is freely supplied with energy. Although the energetics do not immediately concern us, the assembly embodies one or many more or less regular modes of dissipating the energy – steam expansion or metabolism – as a result of which it produces an unlimited supply of observable events.

The Consequences of Uncertainty

When we say that our uncertainty about the environment has been reduced we mean that a larger number of the behavioural predictions we make are turning out to be right. But I take as

* (17) is a comprehensive textbook dealing with scientific observation.

18

an axiom that our uncertainty about the environment cannot be entirely removed. Any *observation* of the real world is fallible and occupies a definite interval Δt.

On the other hand, *predictions* are always dogmatic (though the dogma can be modified in the light of further evidence). The common usage 'I predict event A with probability 0·8 and event B with probability 0·2', is no exception. This statement is a shorthand version of 'I predict (with certainty) that the value of a variable called the probability of A, namely $p(A)$ equals 0·8, and the value of a corresponding variable for B, namely $p(B)$ equals 0·2'. In other words, we are not predicting events, but certain abstract entities called the probabilities of events which can be variously interpreted, for example, in the present case, as an assertion that if either A or B (but no other event) were able to occur upon many occasions, 80 per cent of the time the occurence would be A, and 20 per cent of the time it would be B. Thus, it follows from our axiom, that we do not make predictions about a piece of the real world, an 'assembly' as such, which is unknowable in detail. Rather, we make predictions about some simplified abstraction from the real world – some incomplete image – of which we can become certain (the probability model is, of course, an abstraction of this kind). Subject to some important qualifications, which will appear in the discussion, this simplified abstraction is a 'system'.

The Type of Uncertainty
What is an observer uncertain about? In the first place an observer, absurd as it sounds, may be uncertain about his objective, that is, about the kind of predictions he wishes to make. This is rarely the case so far as a scientific observer is concerned. A scientist usually knows whether he wants to make clinically useful observations, commercially useful observations, or observations compatible with the hypothetico-deductive structure of physics. On the other hand, there are cases of dilettante observation, where the objective is not obvious at the outset and only becomes so when some tentative knowledge has been gained. This situation is not readily analysed, for we can only speak about a source of uncertainty relative to some objective or other, i.e. clinical, commercial or physical prediction

making and for the moment we shall deal exclusively with those cases where the objective *is* specified.

Secondly, an observer with an objective has a structural uncertainty about the kind of assembly he is dealing with and the measurements that are relevant. Take, for example, a brain and the objective of investigating the auditory mechanism. The observer is uncertain about the anatomical regions that perform various computations and even about the validity of dividing the auditory mechanism into functional parts. In turn, he is uncertain of the inquiries to make about a brain; where, for example, to place the recording electrodes.

Structural uncertainty about metabolism entails ignorance of the hierarchical arrangement of the enzymes which catalyse the reaction; or, at a deeper level, about whether enzymes are the active catalysts. Structural uncertainty about an industry is ignorance of the flow diagram to represent the interchange of energy, goods or information.

Finally, supposing the observer has some structure and thus some set of relevant measurements in mind, he is liable to metrical uncertainty about the values of these measurements. (*See Appendix 1.*)

As a case in point, there is a moderately good picture of what happens when a nerve impulse travels along a fibre, but physiologists would like to know more about the effect which is exerted when the impulse reaches a synaptic connection between the fibre and the cell body of another neurone. Our structural notions of impulse transmission suggest measuring the depolarization of the cell membrane in the synaptic region and it is possible to obtain a very accurate measurement of the electrical potential of a micro-electrode inserted into the region concerned. But this, of course, is only an index of the measurement required. The potential itself depends upon a number of unknown quantities and although the observer is sure enough concerning the measurement he ought to make (membrane depolarization) and sure about the value of the index which is technically available (micro-electrode potential) he remains uncertain about the value of the relevant measurement. Indeed, according to our initial axiom, an observer is bound to accept some minimum uncertainty from one source or another, structural uncertainty or metrical uncertainty or both. We shall rationalize the axiom in a rough and ready fashion by noting that the more detailed an observer's structural knowledge the more difficult are the measurements he is impelled to make

The Source of Uncertainty

Uncertainty stems from ourselves and our contact with the world. A real observer is able to recognize some, but not all, possible forms of behaviour. These recognizable forms are his percepts and there is a finite set of them. We have all experienced the sensation 'I can't put my finger on anything'. Of course, we mean that there is no form that we are able to recognize, not that there is no form to be recognized.* Our ideas of chaos come from percepts we have available, which, from our point of view, are not chaotic, or, alternatively, from conventions,† which have been accepted. From the whole gamut of orders that appear in the world we can recognize only a few and these we can only assimilate at a limited rate, through observations at Δt apart.

Whilst the ultimate restriction is imposed by our own capabilities, we are commonly up against other and artificial difficulties. Because of these the object of the study appears to be enclosed in a container, the so called 'Black Box', to which we, as observers, have incomplete access. A 'Black Box'[16] situation gives rise to either structural or metrical uncertainty or both. In the simplest case, the assembly, a piece of electrical equipment, for example, is literally enclosed in a black box with input and output connections.

Tests applied at the input and output yield some information about the equipment, but will not specify its condition unambiguously. Further tests would involve opening the black box and this is disallowed either by a capricious rule or because the equipment must be tested whilst it is functioning (the equipment may be a running dynamo which cannot be stopped for testing). A business efficiency expert allowed to see some, but not all, of a client's books is in a somewhat analogous position. So is an

* We take it, as a matter of *belief*, that the world is such and we are such that we see some order in the world. As Rashevsky [20] puts it, this much must be admitted in order to make science *possible*.

†Such as the convention that a set of uniformly distributed particles is more chaotic than a configured set of particles. Whilst it is a very useful convention, there is nothing sacrosanct about this, as Beer has pointed out."

ecologist who, in order to study the interactions within an animal community, is bound to interfere with the ecological balance.

Individuals circumvent their imperfections by forming a simplified abstraction of the real world, through learning and concept formation (as a result of which, amongst other things, they learn to recognize new percepts). This abstraction, of course, is a private image, but it allows them to deal with and decide about their environment. On the other hand, just because of our human limitations there is advantage to be gained if a group of observers, anxious to make the same sort of predictions, communicate with one another and in place of many private images, build up one commonly understood abstraction (such as the hypothetico-deductive structure of science). This will be a public image of the world within which all observations are assimilable and in terms of which behavioural predictions are made. An observer who subscribes to the plan, must limit himself to observations that are mutually intelligible and which can be assimilated. Again, the rules of deduction which apply in the abstract structure (and on the basis of which these predictions are made) must be rules which have met with public approval.

Definition of a System

We are now in a position to discuss a system of which the simplified abstraction we have examined is a particular case. In the first place, a system entails an a priori *structure* which specifies the logical possibilities an observer can talk about. We shall call it a 'universe of discourse' and will denote it as U. Sometimes U is a loosely related collection of names for objects or events. At the other extreme U is an elaborate mathematical model wherein names are related by manipulable calculi, so that given one relation many others are deducible. In either case, its names and relations and its deductive content (the 'logically true' statements possible in U) exist in the observer's mind independently of any assembly whatever. U does depend upon the observer's previous experience, his objective and his hunch about a useful form of description.

Secondly, a system entails an identification L between the names in U and those attributes of the assembly which the observer regards as relevant to his objective. Hence L specifies the set of possible observations. At one extreme L is defined by a statement like 'I am looking out of an aeroplane window at cloud shadows fleeting over the ground (I recognize shapes distinguished by the categorical attributes "angular", "bulbous" and so on)'. In this case the 'system' is no more than a concept of the cloud configurations, for the attributes are not wholly communicable. At the other extreme L is the precise specification of a reproducible experiment that a potential is measured to the nearest millivolt at point x, a pressure at point y and so on. In this case the 'system' is a public abstraction since the attributes potential and pressure are commonly understood. As a result of the identification the logically true statements in U become plausible hypotheses about the relevant and observable attributes of the assembly and we shall call the pair U, L, a reference frame.[21] (*See Appendix 2.*)

The reference frame itself is a system. It satisfies a definition proposed by Colin Cherry[23] that a system is an 'ensemble of attributes'. But it has no predictive value. In order to show how it becomes of predictive value we shall first introduce a convention for representing U, L, called a 'phase space'. Secondly, we shall credit the observer with a special objective v_1, namely to make predictions about any *behaviour* in U, L. In other words, to discover all he can about a given way of looking at the assembly. Although 'special' v_1 is shared by nearly all 'scientific observers'. Perhaps it is also true that we are impelled to adopt v_1 by a belief in the underlying regularity of the world, and that this regularity will be apparent in the reference frame we have chosen.

Phase Space

Suppose the observer can unambiguously describe his attributes. If he can, his senses can be replaced by instruments which convert events from the assembly into numerically valued attribute variables (including, possibly, two valued variables which equals 1, if an attribute is present and equals 0 if it is absent), labelled $x_1, x_2, \ldots x_m$ and displayed in a common modality (perhaps on dials or meters). In the simplest case, the observer knows very little about the assembly. It is a black box with m initially unrelated outputs. By the usual convention, we represent these outputs, the values of the x variables, as independent co-ordinates in a *phase space*. If $m = 2$ the phase space will be a plane, as in Figure 1, if $m = 3$ a cube, and if $m = 4$ a four-dimensional space.

The phase space is U. The chosen set of m instruments *determine* L. We now define the *state* of the system at any instant t as $X(t) = x_1(t), x_2(t), \ldots x_m(t)$, that is, as an instantaneous observation of all relevant attributes. Now $X(t)$ is a point in U located by marking off observed values of the attribute variables along the co-ordinates of U. Observations can be made no more often than each Δt. Since no absolute value is assigned to Δt, we may as well say $\Delta t = 1$. In this case a *behaviour* of the

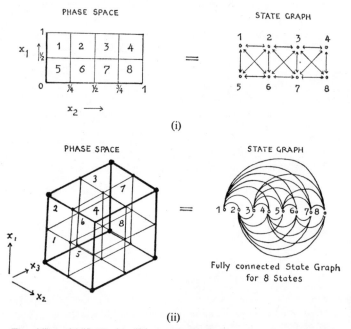

Figs. 1(i) *and* 1(ii). Each cell in a quantised phase space is represented by a single point in the equivalent state graph. Points are connected by lines with arrows showing possible transitions. Since the state need not change, a line should emerge from each point and return. These lines are omitted, for clarity.

system is a sequence of states $X(0)$, $X(1)$ ..., observable at $t = 0, 1, ...$

Because of the observer's metrical uncertainty, observation cannot be exact. Hence the dials may as well be marked in units, an intermediate reading counting as the nearest marked figure. In this case, the phase space is quantized into unit cells, and a real observation can locate the state point within a cell, but with no greater precision. Given these modifications, the state transition graph of Figure 1 (i) is equivalent to the phase space.

Notice, some structure has been introduced with our phase space. It was tacitly assumed that the number '2' on a dial means a greater value than the number '1', that '3' is greater than '2' and '4' than '3'. As a result, some transitions are prohibited in the state graph (compare it with Figure 1 (ii)). Maybe this determines too structured a U (it might, if the attributes described cloud shadows). In this case, the observer could resort to a set of two valued variables, which merely indicated the existence of an attribute. For the same number of variables there are, of course, fewer states, but as in Figure 1 (ii) any state transition is possible. On the other hand, if the observer knows something about the structure of the assembly beforehand he will choose a more structured U, for example, he may know that all possible behaviours carry a state point along a line or between a pair of lines and if so, he can restrict his system to this region of U, L.

Finally, as a point of nomenclature, when we do adopt the state graph picture it seems more natural to talk about state *transitions*, or state *selections*, occurring in discrete jumps rather than behaviours leading the state point along a given path.

Procedure of an Observer with Objective v_1

A system of predictive value is constructed in U, L, through the empirical confirmation or denial of hypotheses. Each hypothesis which tallies with an observation is tentatively 'proven', embodied in U, and its deductive consequences worked out to suggest further hypotheses for testing. (From this point efforts are made to *disprove* tentatively accepted hypotheses.)

The observer is mostly concerned with predictive hypotheses about behaviour, that have the form, 'given the locus of $X(t)$ is A, the locus of $X(t + 1)$ is B'. Such behavioural predictions are advanced by the observer whenever the events in the assembly move the state point in U, and they are tested by observing the subsequent behaviour of the state point. (This is the effort to disprove current hypothesis.) But when a prediction is consistently confirmed and never denied, it acquires the status of an empirical truth on a par with logically true statements in U (such as 'an attribute cannot have two values at once' or 'to get from $x_1 = 1$ to $x_1 = 5$, you must pass through values $x_1 = 2$, $x_1 = 3, x_1 = 4$'). In this case the behaviour is regarded as entirely predictable and it can be embodied in a rule, or *behavioural equation* (or alternatively it can be described by a behavioural path in U). Any entirely predictable behaviour is called state determined, and, by definition, an observer with objective v_1 tries to specify as many state determined behaviours in U, L as possible. Strictly speaking, an inductive procedure like this can never lead to certainty, for, though a single negative case denies an hypothesis, no number of positive cases entirely confirm it.[24] Thus, we assume that at some point the observer becomes confident that some of his predictions, which have never before been denied, never will be denied.

Measurement of Uncertainty and of Information Conveyed
Given a well-defined set of elements, it is possible to measure the *amount* of uncertainty with reference to this set. The reference frame provides a set of states, hence a measure of uncertainty is possible and is called the *variety* of the set. The simplest case is the system in Figure 1 (ii), where, at any instant, each state is equally likely to occur. Since there are n states, an observer is initially uncertain about 'which of n', or conversely, the appearance of one particular state removes this uncertainty and conveys an 'amount of information', selecting one of n possibilities. Information and uncertainty, if expressed in an additive form as logarithmic measures, are very simply related indeed,

$$\text{Uncertainty} = - \text{Information}$$

Because of this, observation can either be thought of as 'removing uncertainty' about a set of possibilities, or selections from the set of possibilities can be thought of as a 'source of information'. We thus define the variety as $+\text{Log.}_2 n$ or the information initially conveyed per observation as $-\text{Log.}_2 n$. As the observer, using v_1, learns and as his system becomes of predictive value, the information conveyed by the appearance of an event is reduced, he can predict what will occur. If the system becomes entirely predictable, and all behaviours state determined, when there is no uncertainty about it, the information is reduced to 0. So we must be careful to distinguish:

(1) The variety of the chosen reference frame U, L, which remains for n unrestricted states always $\text{Log.}_2 n$ per observation. (The variety in Figure 1 (i) is less due to the restrictions of the phase space.)

(2) The variety of the system which the observer builds up in this reference frame (or the variety measured with reference to the observer), which is initially $\text{Log.}_2 n$, but which is reduced as the system becomes of predictive value. If you like, the number of possibilities contemplated by the observer $= n^*$ are reduced and the system variety $= \text{Log.}_2 n^*$.

There is no measurable variety of the assembly, or of the states of the assembly, for in neither case is there a well-defined set of possibilities. In order to have any measurable variety there must be an agreed reference frame.

3 The State Determined Behaviour

A BEHAVIOUR is state determined* if an observer, knowing the
state at t, is able to predict the state at $t + 1$ with certainty.
Rephrased; a behaviour is state determined if $X(t + 1)$ depends
in a unique fashion upon $X(t)$ and, in the phase space, this
means that the path describing a state determined behaviour
does not bifurcate.

We describe the path by a behavioural equation: $X(t + 1) = X(t) \cdot E$. Where E is the transformation in co-ordinates x (the
mathematical instruction for changing point $X(t)$ into $X(t+1)$).
If the behaviour described by this equation is state determined
E is a *closed, single valued* transformation, that is, the next state
is always one of the states in the phase space and the next state
is always uniquely specified.

For the state transition graph, the behavioural equation is
expressed in an equivalent but slightly different form. The states
are labelled $1, 2, \ldots n$. If the behaviour is state determined one
state is unambiguously defined at each instant, hence the state of
the graph is specified, at an instant t, by a binary number $J(t)$,
having n entries indexed by the state labels. Of these entries
$n-1$ are always 0 and one entry, with index corresponding to
the current state, is 1. If $n = 4$, for example, and the second
state is current at $t = 0$, the number $J(0) = 0, 1, 0, 0$. A behaviour
is a sequence of binary numbers:

$$J(0) \longrightarrow J(1) \ldots\ldots\ldots J(r)$$
such as $0, 1, 0, 0, \rightarrow 0, 0, 1, 0, \ldots\ldots 1, 0, 0, 0.$

So the state transition at each step, if the system is state determined, will be a *closed, single valued, selective operation F* upon
$J(t)$ written as $J(t + 1) = J(t) \cdot F$.

Since each entry $J_i(t)$ in the binary number $J(t)$ is in one to

* Much of this chapter reflects the views of Ashby and his detailed
argument should be consulted.[9; 13] Detailed references will not be given.

28

one correspondence, by indexing, with a state X_i it is not difficult to see that the two forms of the behavioural equation are equivalent.

It is more convenient to express a state determined behaviour as powers of a transformation than as a sequence of separate operations. Thus, in the phase space, the state at $t = 2$, $X(2) = X(1) \cdot E = X(0) \cdot E \cdot E = X(0) \cdot E^2$, or in general, at $t = r$, $X(r) = X(0) \cdot E^r$. Similarly, in the state graph, $J(r) = J(0) \cdot F^r$. Where E^r, F^r are the r-th powers of the transformation E, F, and represent concisely that the operation has been repeated upon r successive occasions.

Equilibrium Behaviour

A moment's consideration will convince you that (since the path must be unique) a state determined behaviour must either converge, as in Figure 2, to a fixed state called the 'equilibrium point', or enter a behavioural cycle' as in Figure 3. Either mode of behaviour is called a stable equilibrium because, unless there is some disturbance which moves the state point (or alters the subsequent transformation), its behaviour remains invariant.

Fig. 2. Stable point in a phase space – arrows converge

NOTE: We use the convention of showing a few representative behaviours in the phase space, by single lines. In fact, there are indefinitely many lines.

Mathematically this is due to a property of the powers of E and F, namely that for some $r = 1, 2, \ldots$ and for some $l = 1, 2, \ldots$ with $n > l$. $E^r = E^{r+l}$ and $F^r = F^{r+l}$.

Thus, if $l = 1$, we have the equilibrium 2 and if $l > 1$ we have the equilibrium 3 represented by the sequences:

$$X(r) = X(r + 1) = \ldots \text{ or } J(r) = J(r + 1) = \ldots \text{ for } 2$$

and by
$$X(r) \rightarrow X(r+1) \ldots X(r+l) = X(r) \text{ or}$$
$$J(r) \neq J(r+1) \ldots J(r+l) \neq J(r)$$
with
$$X(r) \neq X(r+1) \text{ and } J(r) \neq J(r+1)^* \text{ for 3.}$$

Fig. 3. A cycle

Since this is true of any state determined behaviour and since a state determined system is made up of state determined behaviours, we *define* a state determined system *as a collection of L identified state determined behaviours which converge to a stable equilibrium in a given U* (the system may be all of these or only some) and it is demarked as a stable region in the phase space, as shown in Figure 4.

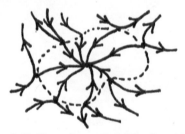

Fig. 4. Stable region enclosed by dotted line

Not all equilibria are stable. A ball balanced on a pin, shown abstractly in Figure 5, is in unstable equilibrium because the slightest disturbance will displace it irreversibly. On the other hand, a ball resting in a hollow is in stable equilibrium *providing* that the disturbances able to push it around are not large enough to move it over the edge of the hollow. (Instability is associated

* For any equilibrial state the selective operation F is a permutation of the position of the '1' in $J(t)$. This includes the identity permutation that leaves '1' in the same position and corresponds to the equilibrium point.

with the uncontrolled dissipation of energy: stability with achievement of an energy minimum, and cyclic activity with controlled dissipation. It is helpful to think in this way, providing that we keep in mind that the behaviour in a phase space is an account of observable events and makes no direct comment upon the energetic aspects of the assembly.)

Fig. 5. Unstable point – arrows diverge.

Except in the 'pure' case, where the system is wholly isolated and there are no disturbances the distinction between stable and unstable equilibria is one of degree rather than kind. But these are useful concepts and their imperfections need not trouble us too much for we shall rarely encounter the 'pure' case of an isolated and state determined system. The great majority of systems have many equilibria. Displacement of the state point from one equilibria may lead (i) to another, or (ii), to some condition, true enough an equilibrium but one which the observer cannot discern for it is outside *U, L*. This, if you like, is real instability for nothing can be said about it.

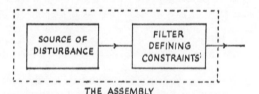

THE ASSEMBLY

Fig. 6. To an observer the assembly enclosed by a dotted line looks like the simulated model shown inside.

Working Models and Relations between Systems
A reference frame is chosen and imposed upon the assembly by the observer and from his point of view the assembly 'black

box' could be replaced by a literally constructed 'black box' which includes some device for producing the events which are manifest as motions of the state points in U and some filtering mechanism which selects the events of admissible behaviours (from the set of all possible events). I have shown the observer's eye view in Figure 6 and it is essential to notice that the filtering mechanism summarizes only those constraints in the assembly which act upon the relevant attributes (not all the constraints that exist). Because of this any system forms the basis for a working model or simulation of some facets of many different assemblies and it is irrelevant what the model is made from. Commonly, for example, working models are made using electrical analogue computers and their logic is identical with the observer's eye view of Figure 6. The box of constraints, the filtering mechanism, is some arrangement of parts in the computer which, physically speaking, has equilibria that correspond to the abstract equilibria, and behaviours that correspond to abstract behaviours. The model is set in motion to generate all possible behaviours by an auxiliary mechanism which feeds energetic disturbances into the constraint box. In our abstract picture, of course, these correspond with displacements of the state point. But precisely the same arrangement of parts in the computer can represent the spread of an epidemic, the spread of rumours in a community,[22] the development of rust on a piece of galvanized iron, and diffusion in a semi-conductor.

It is natural to ask how models and systems are related. In the case of models the answer is easy, for we have explicitly neglected the choice of L. If two models, such as the 'epidemic' and the 'rumour' model are mathemically identical, we say they are *isomorphic*. If they differ only with respect to detail, for example, if each cycle in the first corresponds with an equilibrium in the second, we say that the second model is a *homomorph* of the first (strictly, if the second is a mapping of the first which preserves the group operation of the state transformation – here matrix multiplication). Now the second, homomorphic model, is also the observer's eye view of an observer who had thrown away some of the available information (in a carefully calculated manner, so that his image is less detailed than but consistent with the original). So, in this sense, we can say that two systems are isomorphic or homomorphic. But, is this useful? On these

i)   (ii)

PLATE I (i) Simulating a pupil-teacher system. Solartron EUCRATES II (see page 67).

(ii) Murray Babcock's adaptive reorganising automaton. Network connections are made by plugged leads between 'neurone' and 'synapse' sockets. State is displayed on a neon tube matrix (see page 67).

(iii) A practical evolutionary system. Learning machine is marked 'A' and thread structures are developed in dishes marked 'B'. This demonstration was set up by the author at the Symposium on the Mechanisation of Thought Processes, held at the National Physical Laboratory, November, 1958.

(iii)

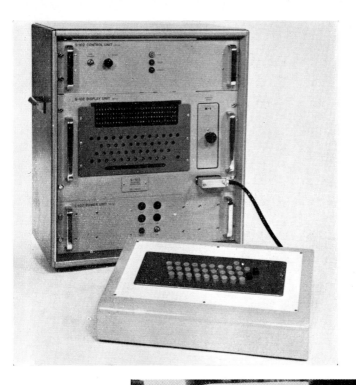

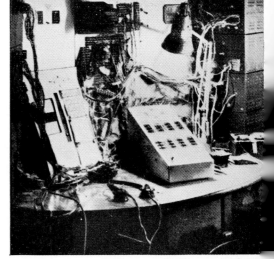

PLATE II (*Above*).
Automatic keyboard
instructor: Solar-
tron SAKI (see page
96). (*Below*) Main-
tenance training
teaching machine.
Assembly photo-
graphed in the
author's own
laboratory (see page
90)

grounds a system representing the motion of a roundabout is isomorphic with a circular argument. True, they both entail the idea of going round, but that is the content of the isomorphism and I am not entirely certain what it means. For the states of the roundabout are not only different from the states of an argument, they are described in a different and, at the moment, incomparable language. I am disinclined to accept the utility of mathematical relations between such states or the corresponding systems. On the other hand, I am prepared to say that the systems representing the 'epidemic', 'rumour', 'rust' and 'semi-conductor' assemblies are isomorphic because, although the states are different, we can talk about them in the same language and compare the L determined measurements we make.

According to this view, a pair of systems are comparable if the L of their reference frames are comparable. In particular, systems in the same reference frame must be comparable, and this fact allows us to give a rigorous expression to the blackness of the black box. Any state determined system is the homomorph of some more detailed system which is also state determined. Ultimately, if we believe in the underlying regularity of an assembly, there is a state determined system of immense detail which, due to our imperfections, we cannot directly observe.

Object Language and Metalanguage

For the rest of the discussion we shall adopt an omniscient attitude and look externally upon the observer and his black box. We are now talking about the observer rather than seeing the world through his eyes, and, of course, we talk in different terms. Since we shall use this gambit and others like it a good deal, I shall call the observer's language an *object language*[23] (with words that refer to states in his reference frame) and our language (in terms of which we talk about an observer) the *metalanguage*. I am introducing the distinction at this point because it will be convenient if we can look inside the observer's black box and know in greater detail than he does what kind of assembly there is. To keep something tangible in mind I propose that the assembly is actually a town, with the road plan of Figure 7, and the attribute variables are actually meters that read the number of motor vehicles residing at a given instant upon the labelled intersections in Figure 7. The observer is trying to make sense of what we call 'traffic flow', and, in practice, when the box is not completely black, he may be more or less aware that this is his job in life. Now, in this case, when we are talking about 'an observer', both the metalanguage and the object language are well determined.

There is a second innovation. So far we have thought of

Fig. 7. A black box and its interior

observers who merely receive the events generated by an assembly. But most observers are not content to watch and wait. They act upon the assembly and induce the system to change states in a satisfying manner. Thus, a dog is stimulated in a Pavlovian conditioning experiment; a patient, guided by his physician, energizes his own implanted electrodes and reports the results, and our traffic observers may be allowed to create a local influx of motor vehicles or connect up traffic signals. Notice, they need have no more knowledge of *what they are doing* than they have of *what they are measuring*. But *we* know omnisciently. The logical position is that an observer of this kind, a so-called *participant* observer,[21] is provided with a set of labelled buttons in addition to his labelled dials. These buttons are his possible actions, and he is told, at least, that each action induces some cogent change of state in the system. But it is a necessary digression to point out that this is not always the case. (In particular it is not when we discuss the interaction between real life students and adaptive machines.) If two people are in conversation, for example, their discourse takes place in an object language and we make comments about the conversation in a metalanguage, possibly in terms of psychology. These comments are objective, but the object language itself may be concealed. We do not know the participants' reference frame. Words have implications for the *participants*, of which *we* are unaware and, in general, we cannot expect to make objective measurements of the interaction, i.e. we cannot measure the information from one participant to another.

Partitioning Systems

Suppose, speaking omnisciently, we know that motor vehicles do not start or stop in town, but aim for the throughway by the quickest route, that traffic flows into A and B of Figure 7, and that the rate of inflow is such that a stationary distribution of motor vehicles will be built up over a relatively short interval. In these conditions x_1, x_2, x_3, x_4 and x_5 will assume positive values and probably change, but x_6, x_m will be zero valued. We assume also that the traffic flow from A exerts no appreciable effect upon the traffic flow from B (the throughway is a wide road and the traffic signal connections are not made). An observer, possibly ignorant of all the mechanism involved but observing the variables, will remark there are two substantially independent subsystems (namely, $\alpha = x_1, x_2, x_3$ and $\beta = x_4, x_5$). In other words, he *partitions* the variables into two subsets one which *we know* refers to A and the other to B. Partitioning is one important way to reduce the elaboration of a gigantic system with vast numbers of equilibria. The gambit works whenever there are structural constraints such as the components in a computer, different processes in a factory, different tissues in an animal or different traffic streams in a town.

The phrase 'subsystem' is natural enough if we happen to know that the subset of variables refer to streams of traffic. But a partitioned subset of variables is closely related also to our concept of a '*machine*'* (not necessarily a collection of physical parts but any entity which does a specific job). The relation is of this kind. Suppose the participant observer could change x_1 and x_2 at will (these variables being called the 'input' to the 'machine' α) then x_3, which is called the 'output' of the 'machine' α would change in a definite way. Commonly we say the output is a mathematical function of the input and in electronic machines it is often dubbed the transfer function: $x_3 = f_1(x_1, x_2)$ which, given the extremely stringent conditions assumed a moment ago, reduces to $x_3 = x_1 + x_2$. In this case we know that α is a 'machine for changing the distribution of motor vehicles', and it is tempting to say α is 'the road layout'. But this would be wrong. α is what the road layout actually does, specified by f_1. An observer need know nothing about motor vehicles and still see the same machine, only he might call it 'a machine for adding two numbers x_1 and x_2'.

But a participant observer may do more than 'stimulate'. His repertoire of actions is likely to include such things as $C = $ 'Introduce the traffic signal connection with sensing element at a and stop lamps at b. Obviously, this alters f_1 into some other function f_2, plausibly enough into:

$$x_3 = f_2(x_1, x_2) = x_2 + x_1 \cdot (1 - z) \text{ with } z \text{ a positive, fractional constant}$$

* The term 'machine' corresponds with the current usage in this field. A state determined subsystem is equivalent to the most elementary logical paradigm a 'Turing Machine'[26] which has one binary input and one binary output determined by its input and the state of the Turing Machine when the input is applied.

since congestion will occur at the traffic signal stop lamps and a number of motor vehicles proportional to x_1 will filter along D which has become, for them, a most direct route. We call C, or anything that changes f, a 'parameter' of the subsystem or machine.

It must be admitted that the distinction between an 'input' and a 'parameter' is a little arbitrary. When x_1 and x_2 increase in the rush hour f will be changed. If x_6 is given a positive value f will probably change and the observer is at liberty either to define a new system, including x_6 or to regard x_6 as a parameter of α. Then the whole concept of a subsystem is 'arbitrary', in the sense that it depends not only upon the 'regularities' in the assembly which, from omniscience, we know *to exist* but also upon those the observer chooses to *recognize*.

Coupling Systems

Apart from the actions of a participant observer, a subsystem can be affected by the other subsystems. Thus α can be affected by β, in which case we say that α is *coupled* to β. As a result of a coupling the integrity of the subsystems is partly lost. However, it is still useful to distinguish between them if the *manner* of coupling is specified by some function, say g to distinguish it from f. It may be, for example that $g(\beta)$ which relates α to β involves only some of the variables of β or only some of the states of β (coupling is significant only if there is a particular distribution of the traffic). In common with 'actions' the states of β may act as either 'inputs' (as stimuli) or as parameter changes. Whilst admitting that the distinction is tenuous it is still convenient to represent these possibilities separately. Hence, (using our definition of a subsystem, as a relatively isolated functional entity) we show subsystems as boxes and distinguish:

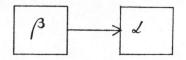

Output state of β acts as input to α

Fig. 8

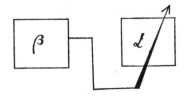

Output state of β changes parameters of α

Fig. 9

remembering in each case that the box does not necessarily imply a collection of physical parts. Of these, Figure 8 may entail coupling the traffic light linkage d, c, of Figure 7 which stops traffic flow along E when x_5 increases beyond a limit, also to lamp b, whereas Figure 9 may entail a device which renders the linkage a, b operative if and only if x_5 exceeds this limit.

If the coupling is two-way, so that β affects α and α affects β. we say that α and β are *interacting*. When the *interaction* is very severely restricted there is some point in talking about feedback as we did in Chapter 1, and analysing the system in terms of feedback theory. But most of the systems that concern us are so elaborate that the techniques of feedback theory are inapplicable. Interaction by feedback makes the sub-systems very hazy and, as mentioned in Chapter 1, gives rise to apparently purposive forms of behaviour.

Of course, from our omniscient viewpoint, the black box and the observer are merely a pair of subsystems; subsystems in our metalanguage, however! In the upper picture, Figure 10 (i) I have tried to show what goes on in these terms when an observer aims for v_1 (to obtain a participant observer connect channel Ξ; to make yourself a plain observer disconnect channel Ξ). The lower picture refers to the next part of our discussion.

Alternative Procedure

There is no guarantee that an observer, using v_1 will achieve a state determined system. Some of the behaviours in his phase space may remain ambiguous, like Figure 11, where A goes sometimes to B and sometimes to C.

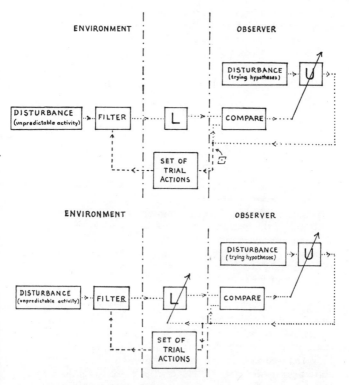

Fig. 10. Different kinds of observation and experimentation viewed as systems

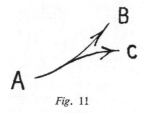

Fig. 11

In this case the observer may either:

(i) Examine a system of greater detail and diversity, so that *A* becomes a pair of states, a_1 which always leads to *B*, and a_2 which always leads to *C* as in Figure 12.

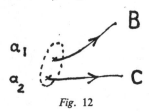

Fig. 12

(ii) Resort to statistical observation.

First of all, let us look at (i). We and possibly the observer know that motor vehicles are being counted. They are discrete entities and, unless the instruments are misfunctioning, they cannot be counted more accurately! So it is only possible to improve the measurements by reducing Δt and counting 'more often'. Even here a useful lower limit is set by the maximum speed of the motor vehicles and we may as well assume that Δt is within the limit. So the observer must look for a greater diversity of data, for example, he must investigate more of the intersections of Figure 7, since $x_1, x_2, \ldots x_m$ are only a subset of the possible measures $x_1, x_2, \ldots x_n$, $n > m$, which are potentially available. This does, of course, entail changing *L* and possibly also *U* (since more, as well as different, variables may be needed to describe a state determined system). Hence, the objective is no longer v_1. Instead, the observer is looking for a state determined system, in *any* reference frame available (and we suppose that this search is permitted). Unless some restriction is imposed, the search will be haphazard. Thus, we assume that the observer wishes to discover a state determined system sufficient to make some specified kind of prediction, for example, sufficient to control the traffic. Any such objective will be called v_2 and the procedure adopted by an observer will have the form 'Choose a reference frame U_1, L_1 and test for a state determined system in U_1, L_1, but if this is not achieved after a certain arbitrary effort, choose a further reference frame U_2, L_2 and if necessary another U_3, L_3, and another U_4, L_4 and so on'. (Figure 10 (ii).) Whilst the procedure for v_1 was essentially a matter of chance trial, v_2 is likely to involve the elements of insight and invention. This becomes obvious when we consider the L an observer may choose. If the single attribute 'number of motor vehicles' provides insufficient evidence he may take the make and model of the motor vehicles into account or, for that matter, the drivers' occupations, the plays that are running in town, or the day of the week.

Statistical Determinacy

Suppose that the observer is not allowed this latitude. His instruments are given and he must stick to the method of Figure 10 (i). Since he cannot split A into a_1 and a_2, he may have to give up in despair. On the other hand, it may be possible to neglect some of the detailed state changes and make consistent statistical assertions. But, this possibility depends very much upon the assembly, and an observer can in no way guarantee success.

If he looks long enough for many, say 100, transitions to take place from state A in Figure 12 an observer may be able to conclude:

(i) That A always went either to B or to C.
(ii) That it went into B 80 times, and C 20 times, out of 100.

To summarize the information he writes proportions $\eta_{AB} = 0.8$ and $\eta_{AC} = 0.2$. These empirical estimates of the transition probabilities from state A to state B, and state A to state C, were obtained by 'time averaging' the results.

There is, however, a basically different way to glean statistical data. Suppose there are many, say 100, observers looking at different, but macroscopically similar, assemblies in the same reference frame. If 80 of them report simultaneously, perhaps, that A goes into B and 20 of them report that A goes into C, this knowledge may also be summarized by proportions $\mu_{AB} = 0.8$ and $\mu_{AC} = 0.2$, which are also empirical estimates of transition probabilities, obtained in this case by a process of 'averaging over an ensemble of systems'. But an ensemble average is possible if and *only* if the reference frame U, L is commonly agreed, and the observers are in a position to agree about what assemblies *are* macroscopically similar. Traffic observers, perhaps, are unlikely to employ an ensemble average, but the device is often used in psychology (80 subjects passed a test, 20 failed a test) and in any case we need the concept for our later discussion.

Returning to the single observer: if on repeated inspection the values of η_{AB} and η_{AC} do not change he will become convinced that there is an underlying statistical constraint because of which these proportions exist. In other words, he uses the consistency of η_{AB} and η_{AC} as empirical evidence in favour of an hypothesis that there is regularity in the world, and infers the existence of a statistical structure (which determines the detailed behaviour somewhere within the black box). Suppose, that for each state $i = 1, 2, \ldots n$ and $j = 1, 2, \ldots n$, it is true that empirical estimates η_{ij} are unchanging, an observer may legitimately infer a set of related statistical constraints that determine a *statistical system*. Because the estimates are invariant the statistical system is said to be a *stationary system*. One important consequence of stationarity is that for long enough or large enough samples $\eta_{ij} = \mu_{ij} \rightarrow p_{ij}$, where p_{ij} represents an actual statistical constraint which determines the transition probability from state i to state j.

It is wise to be wary of the concept 'stationary statistical system'. It allows us to predict the range of behaviour of a single observable system or the range of behaviour manifest amongst an ensemble of observable systems, given that the constraints p_{ij} do exist. But statements about it have no tangible referent. They refer to a set of observables not any one. However, in so far as the observer's inference of stationary valued transition probabilities p_{ij} is valid, the statistical system is necessarily of a kind called 'Markovian', and in a sense which we shall discuss, any 'Markovian' system is statistically determinate.

Markovian Systems

The probability that a Markovian system will occupy each of its states at $t + 1$, depends only upon its state at t, and probabilistic transformation P made up of fixed transition probabilities p_{ij}. The state of a state determined system at $t + 1$ depends only upon its state at t, and a fixed state transformation. The obvious correspondence between these two assertions impels us to say that the Markovian system is statistically determinate, indeed the state determined system with transformation F, is a special case of the Markovian system, achieved by replacing the probabilities p_{ij} in P, by certainties. Since inductive procedures do not lead to complete certainty it is, perhaps, better to say that all systems are statistical. 'Determinate' is the name we give to a system with particularly 'consistent' statistics.

Before going further, let us get rid of an apparent restriction. The states of a Markovian system depend only upon the immediate past, but an observer could perfectly well appreciate much longer-term dependencies. Suppose he does (and that these dependencies are consistent) it is always possible to represent his knowledge in terms of an 'expanded' system which is still 'Markovian', but which has a larger number of possible states. These additional states are time dependent. In place of i and j, we have 'i preceded by i', 'i preceded by j', 'j preceded by i', 'j preceded by j' and so on. A Markovian system is thus rather comprehensive.

It is represented by a state transition graph, as in Figure 1, each pair of states i, j being associated with a transition probability, that is, a number $1 > p_{ij} > 0$. Since some transition must occur at each instant (possibly the transformation of a state into itself) the sum of the probabilities associated with arrows moving away from a state (including the arrow which moves away and returns) must equal 1.

By analogy with F we can construct a probabilistic transformation of the binary number which represents the state of the system at $t = 0$, by summarizing the p_{ij} in a transition probability matrix P. (*See Appendix* 3).

However, the transformation no longer leads to a unique state but to a probability distribution or in other words, a statement for each of the n states of their probabilities of occurrence at $t = 1$, given the state specified at $t = 0$. We call this distribution.

$$p_i(1) = p_{i1}(1), p_{i2}(1), \ldots p_i n(1)$$
and write
$$p_i(1) = J(0)\cdot P, \text{ or since } J(t) \text{ is a special case of } p(t) \text{ with all}$$
entries 1 or 0, $p_i(1) = p_i(0)\cdot P$.

We continue, as with the state determined system but obtaining further distributions
$$p_i(2) = p_i(1)\cdot P = p_i(0)\cdot P^2, \text{ or for } t = r$$
$$p_i(r) = p_i(r-1)\cdot P = p_i(0)\cdot P^r$$

A distribution $p_i(t)$ is the *state* of the *Markovian system* and a sequence of distributions is a *behaviour* of the *Markovian system*, conditional upon the chosen initial state $_i$. Instead of choosing a particular initial state we could have chosen a probability distribution – in particular – if we had chosen the distribution $p_i(0) = \dfrac{1}{n}, \dfrac{1}{n}, \cdots \dfrac{1}{n}$ so that each state is equally likely, the resulting distributions would be the unconditional states of the Markovian system.

We can also construe the statistical transformation as an instruction to take a four-sided, or in general, an n-sided dice and to bias it according to the entries in the row of P which corresponds with our chosen initial state. The dice is thrown and the outcome determines the state at $t = 1$, of a hypothetical, *determinate system* (let us call it a *representative system*) which is one of a statistical ensemble. The row of P selected by this outcome is used to bias the dice for a second throw, the outcome of which selects the state of the *representative system* at $t = 2$, and so on. In the phase space the sequence of states generated by dice-throwing delineates the behaviour of a single *representative system*.

Consider a large number of dice thrown simultaneously, many from each different initial state and each according to these instructions. Each one determines a representative system and is assigned to a point in the phase space (the whole set of state points forming an ensemble). A sequence of throws generates a behaviour of each representative system and the points move. If the number of representative systems, and hence of state points is very large, we can neglect their individual behaviour and consider only the density of points, that is, the behaviour of the ensemble. The behaviour of the ensemble is the behaviour of the Markovian system.

Stochastic Models

Since dice throwing exhibits all possible behaviours, given the statistical constraints of a Markovian system, it is a stochastic model (analogous to a determinate model) for simulating the behaviour of an assembly. The constraints represent stock-holding parameters, demand functions, and value fluctuations (or any other statistically known quantity), pertinent to a business or an industrial process. The simulation is called a Monte Carlo procedure and is programmed on a digital computer. Each *initial state* of the stochastic model corresponds with an *initial displacement* of the determinate model. *Each set* of representative systems started from a given state, corresponds with a *single behaviour* of the determinate model. The point needs emphasis perhaps, because each representative system in the set *is*, of course, a determinate system, which is however state determined by the *dice and* by the *statistical constraints* jointly.

Statistical Equilibrium (*see Appendix 4*)

By analogy with a state determined system any Markovian system reaches statistical equilibrium. In equilibrium it is characterized by averages η_{ij} and, regarded as an information source, it has a measurable variety. For n states, the maximum variety is $\text{Log.}_2 n$, the variety of the reference frame, without any statistical constraints. But by learning about the η_{ij} an observer can reduce the variety of the system, as he sees it, to a minimum figure which depends upon P. This variety is equivalent to Shannon's[28] statistical information measure on the system. It is a maximum when the equilibrium distribution $p^* = \dfrac{1}{n}, \dfrac{1}{n}, \cdots \dfrac{1}{n}$ indeed, in this case, it is $\text{Log.}_2 n$. Unequal probabilities p_i, p_j, reduce the variety. Conditional constraints p_{ij} render the state of the system more predictable and decrease the variety still further, by an amount called the redundancy of the source. (*see Appendix 5.*)

Non-Stationary Systems

Suppose there is an honest to goodness statistical whirligig, with dice throwers and bits and pieces of mechanism to determine the p_{ij}, all enclosed in a black box. The whirligig has n different states and each of these is accessible to an observer – when the model is in a particular state a particular lamp is illuminated. However, it could be rather a subtle device, a 'learning' machine, in which the p_{ij} changed from moment to moment, in which case we write $p_{ij}(t)$ in place of p_{ij} and notice that the output of our learning machine is non-stationary.

Taking an omniscient view, the rules which change the statistical constraints are part of the specification (the rules will have the form '$p_{ij}(t)$ is some mathematical function of the previous states'), and the whole thing, rules and all, is an expanded Markovian system. An observer who looks long enough can make valid estimates η_{ij} of the constraints. 'Memory' or the ability to 'learn' is not a property of the system, but of the relation between the system and an observer. As Ashby points out, any system with many equilibria will exhibit 'memory' if some of its states are indistinct. Of two observers, looking at the same assembly, one – who is able to distinguish few states– will say his system has a 'memory', whereas the other – able to distinguish many states – will say his system has none (*see Appendix* 6).

Discarding omniscience let us look at a black box through the eyes of an observer who can only form estimates η_{ij} of a limited set of states. The behaviour of the system may be wholly intractable. On the other hand, the behaviour may be described by a Markovian system, say P_1, which reaches a temporary stable or metastable equilibrium and remains there for an interval. Then, rather suddenly, the behaviour changes. The new behaviour is represented by a different Markovian system, say P_2, which again reaches a metastable equilibrium, then, in turn, gives place to P_3 and P_4.

Animal learning is a case in point. When primates are learning to solve problems, their behaviour, though not strictly stationary, remains approximately so; the learning curves can be extrapolated with confidence, and the behaviour is predictable. Then, rather suddenly, the creature learns a new concept and subsequently deals with problems in a different way which it sticks to for a further appreciable interval. Once again, the learning curves can be extrapolated and a different kind of behaviour becomes predicable. But in between the two behavioural modes there is a discontinuity and prediction of the subsequent mode, given the initial mode, is impossible unless we make use of averages over an ensemble of animals. H. Harlow, for example[30], distinguishes between repetitive learning which is predictable and the process of concept or 'set' learning which entails discontinuities that can be interpreted as 'insightful' behaviour.

The statistical system we have examined is tractable because, by analogy with a determinate system, it can be partitioned into statistical subsystems. An equivalent black box would contain a whirligig having a set P of possible transition matrices P_i and a selective operation F^* to choose different members of P at different instants. On the other hand, if the system cannot be partitioned (or if the selective operation acts too fast to allow an observer to sample each P_i) the estimates η_{ij} are worthless and the observer must rely upon ensemble averages μ_{ij}.

The difficulty is to decide which systems *are* macroscopically similar. Given a lot of identical molecules, we are on safe ground in saying that 'macroscopically similar' collections are those retained at the same temperature and pressure. But, it is less convincing to hear that 'macroscopically similar' learners are individuals selected from the same breed of rat.

The Self-Organizing System

A non-stationary system becomes 'self-organizing' when there is uncertainty about the criteria of macroscopic similarity. Definitions are offered by Beer[32], Pringle[33], Von Foerster[34], and myself[35] [36]. An observer is impelled to change his criteria of similarity (hence, also, his reference frame) in order to make sense of the self-organizing systems, behaviour and he changes it on the basis of what he has already learned (by his interaction with the system). Typically self-organizing systems are 'alive' though we shall examine some which have been embodied in 'inanimate' materials. Let us take 'man', whom most of us would agree is a self-organizing system. A man is any member of a well-specified set of men. But this set can be well-specified (that is, specified in a way that meets common approval) in a vast number of ways, according to an observer's objective. Man, for example, may be specified anatomically (two legs, head, and so on), or alternatively as a decision maker which influences and is influenced by his circle of acquaintances. Each specification is equally valid and entails criteria of similarity. The point is, there are objectives for which neither the first specification (and the criteria it entails), nor the second (and the criteria it entails) are sufficient. In conversation, when trying to control a man, to persuade him to do something, how do I define him? Manifestly I do not, at least, I continually change my specification in such a way that he appears *to me* as a self-organizing system.

Hence, the phrase 'self-organizing system', entails a *relation between* an observer and an assembly. It also entails the observer's objective (an assembly may be a self-organizing system for one observer but not another, or for one objective but not another). Again it is possible that an assembly will appear as a self-organizing system initially and become stationary after inter-action (the conversation partner does, on average, what I ask him). The dependence is also evident in measures of organization; for example, Von Foerster proposes to use Shannon's Redund-ancy (Appendix 5) for this purpose. A system is 'self-organizing' if the rate of change of its redundancy is positive. From Appendix 5 redundancy is a function of V^* and $Vmax$ (two information measures) of which V^* depends chiefly upon constraints developed within the specified system but $Vmax$ depends upon the specifica-tion and the observer's frame of reference.

4 Control Systems

A CONTROLLER is a natural or constructed assembly which interacts with its environment to bring about a particular stability called the 'goal' or 'objective'. Hence the participant observers are controllers (with 'goals' or 'objectives' v_1 or v_2). Indeed, whenever there is a stable system, then, in principle, we can envisage a subsystem acting as the controller that maintains this stability. More often, though, we come across controllers that have been deliberately built (thermostats, process controllers) and the partitioning which separates these devices from the environment is given by their construction.

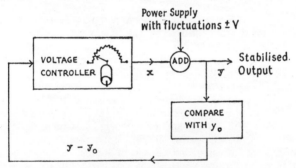

Fig. 13a. A simple controller

The voltage controller of Figure 13a is a case in point*. Physically it is a neat, mechanically distinct entity. The state of its environment is represented by the value of one variable,

* This is a first order linear servo $dy/dt = -b(y-y_0,)$ with b a positive constant. Solving for y we have $y = y_0.(1-e^{-bt})$ thus as t increases y approaches y_0. We shall not discuss the mathematics of servomechanisms because it is a subject in its own right [37]. Reference is made to MacColl and, for applications to behavioural science, in particular, sociology, to Tustin [38].

49

namely the voltage y which is to be stabilized at a chosen value y_0. In the absence of the controller the supply voltage v fluctuates about y_0. To maintain $y = y_0$ a 'difference signal' $y-y_0$ is applied in negative feedback to the controller. Now, from inspection, $y = x + v$ where x is the controller output derived from a potentiometer placed across an auxiliary power source. The 'negative feedback' connection means that the motor which moves this potentiometer is driven at a rate $-(y-y_0)$ hence that the rate of change of x, is equal to $-(y-y_0)$. The controller is in equilibrium if and only if x is unchanging and this is the case only when $y = y_0$, $x = v - y_0$.

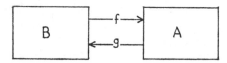

Fig. 13*b*. Abstract image of simple controller

Such a control is formally represented in Figure 13*b* by a subsystem A (the controller) with states X, a subset being equilibrial, a subsystem B, (the environment) with states Y, of which a subset ξ is the objective (i.e., includes the state we want the environment to assume) and coupling functions f and g, whereby A and B interact (i.e. states of A displace states of B and vice versa). The coupling functions and the behavioural equation of A are so chosen that Y is in ξ if and only if X is equilibrial. The behavioural equation of A is often called the controller's 'decision rule' since it determines what corrective displacement attends each change of state in the environment and there is a sense in which A's tendency to equilibrium forces Y into ξ. The formalism adequately describes any 'Automatic' controller like the voltage regulator, (any device which has a fixed 'decision' rule) and any simple homeostasis. In order to design such a thing we must, of course, know what the rule should be (which entails having a model to represent the environment and determine what is and what is not a corrective response).

Not all controllers are so simple. An 'Adaptive' or 'ultrastable'[39] controller is shown, formally in Figure 13*c*. Its designer need not have a comprehensive model of the environment – hence, in the picture, we show a source of unpredictable disturbances per-

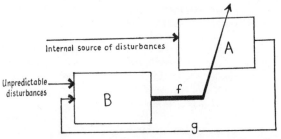

Fig. 13c. Abstract image of adaptive or ultrastable controller

turbing the states of *B*. Nor is there a unique decision rule. Instead there is a set of possible rules – possible state transformations. An internal source of disturbances perturbs the state of *A*, (as designers, we should say that this source induces *A* to make trial actions). Now whatever rule (or transformation) is currently selected we know, from our previous arguments, that the behaviour of *A* on its own would be equilibrial. If this equilibrial behaviour also forces *Y* into ξ then the system as a whole is equilibrial and the currently selected decision rule is left unchanged. On the other hand, if the whole (*A* and *B* interacting) does not reach equilibrium, the rule (or a 'state' transformation) is changed and the process is repeated until equilibrium is achieved.

Important Restrictions

(i). The controller in Figure 13a *is stable and successful only for a limited range of fluctuations.* If *v* goes plus or minus too much, *x* does also, and the potentiometer arm comes off the end of its winding, which is an irreversible change. If *v* changes too fast the motor cannot keep pace and the controller fails to correct the fluctuation which may lead to cumulative instability.

(ii). *The variety of actions must be at least as great as the variety of the fluctuations to be corrected.*

This principle, which Ashby calls 'requisite variety' is most strikingly illustrated if we suppose:

I. The potentiometer replaced by a switch (this is no travesty, for a real potentiometer *is like* a switch and *x* does change in discrete units).

II. That v also assumes discrete values. In this case, switch positions (controller's actions) select columns in the table of Figure 13d and values of v select rows. The states of the environment, now more conveniently called outcomes, are the entries in the table. For convenience, it is assumed that $y_0 = 0$ when the outcomes 0 become the set ζ. Since the potentiometer only moves one right, one left, or stays where it is in each interval Δt the selective variety per Δt is $\text{Log.}_2 3$.

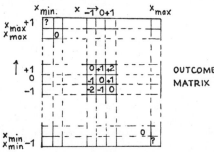

OUTCOME MATRIX

Fig. 13d. Outcome matrix used to determine a decision rule.

If the same restrictions apply to disturbances occurring no more often than once per Δt the environment variety is also $\text{Log.}_2 3$ and, by inspection, whatever value v assumes the controller can maintain an outcome $= 0$ in ζ. On the other hand, if v changes more rapidly, say, two moves per Δt, this is no longer the case, nor is it the case for magnitudes greater than $v = x_{max}$ or less than $v = x_{min}$. 'Requisite variety' applies equally for any well-defined set of actions and outcomes and changes in the environment. (Since in the general case, the entries are unrestricted the 'table' is isomorphic with the 'outcome matrix' which, in the theory of games, specifies the outcome attending a pair of moves, one by each of two participants selecting columns j and rows i respectively. In the theory of games a number θ_{ij} is assigned, for each participant, to each entry and the matrix of numbers is called the pay-off matrix, for it says how much of some desirable commodity each participant receives for each possible combination of moves. The present participants are A and B. It is feasible to assign number θ_{ij}, related in some way to achievement of ξ to each outcome and thus determine a pay-off matrix. We have, in fact, done this in our table. But whereas the numbers in the table lead to a rather obvious decision rule, the decision rule for the general case is far from obvious.)

III. *To extend the principle, 'The amount of control (measured as a variety) depends upon the amount of information the controller gleans from its environment'.* In stating 'requisite variety' we assumed that A had complete information about B (regarded as a participant, A could inspect B moves and the pay-off matrix, before selecting an A move). Commonly, of course, the system B is enclosed in a 'black box' (A receiving imperfect evidence about B). Hence, we distinguish two kinds of controller – the simple 'perfectly informed' type, and 'imperfectly informed' controllers which we shall discuss in a moment.

IV. A voltage controller acts *in a well-defined reference frame of voltage at c*. It cannot appreciate voltages other than at c, it is notoriously unable to deal with humidity changes which exert a very adverse effect upon its behaviour and it reacts rather badly to kicks. This is *not true* of every controller. Biological controllers, in particular, can change their reference frame (*see* Chapter 7).

Automatic Controllers

Automatic controllers receive perfect information about the system they control and have fixed decision rules, that determine their actions. They are the stuff that automation used to be, and sometimes still is, made from. Personally I am more impressed by pianolas and calliopes than any grim automaton running a production line. Do not despize the machines even if you cannot spare my childish wonderment. I have seen a kind of pianola made in 1920, which includes a fourth order non-linear servo system, and the most elaborate code transformation from the input music roll. These beautiful machines reached a peak of ingenuity years ago and, for all the talk, automation, in the classical sense, is a hoary old art. The best place to learn it is in the music hall, beside Sutros, on the cliff at San Francisco. The second best place is Disneyland – I admit a preference for northern California. In England we have Battersea Park.

Typically, an industrial controller senses a certain combination of events, for example, that all of r different welding procedures have been completed, upon the n-th piece of metalwork at booth i, via a logical network. As a result of this information, the automatic controller takes an action determined by its decision rule, i.e. moves the n-th job to booth $i + 1$. It then awaits the $r + 1$th event, a feedback signal to say the metalwork has arrived, after which it is free to accept the $n + 1$th job at booth i, and the whole cycle is repeated. The automatic controller is inert. If the metalwork runs out it does nothing, or at best rings a bell to say it is idle. It cannot prod its environment, looking for work, and, unfortunately, the same is true of my favourite calliopes.

The Distinction between Perfectly and Imperfectly Informed Controllers

In the simplest case a perfectly informed, automatic controller reduces to Figure 14. (i) in which the switch A is turned by the controller to actions α, β, whilst switch B is turned by the behaviour of the environment to stages a, b, at each instant Δt. For the moment we can neglect the small devil G, who alters the structure of the environment, because he is quiescent. According to the circuit, the lamp is illuminated if and only if $A = \alpha$ when $B = a$, and $A = \beta$ when $B = b$, and this is indicated in the pay-off matrix. We shall call the lamp a knowledge of results signal, since it tells the controller the result of its action *after* it has selected an action*. In addition the controller receives complete information about the state of the environment (B switch position) through channel F. Hence, assuming it can select one action each Δt, and given the decision rule $A = \alpha$, if $B = a$, $A = \beta$, if $B = b$, it can keep the lamp illuminated by matching its actions (A switch positions) to the state of the environment. Notice the 'decision rule' entails 'a model' of the environment which, in this case, is *built into* the controller.

---

* Strictly a servomechanism, like the voltage regulator, receives only knowledge of results since it must make some trial displacement in order to elicit a difference signal. Indeed, in the region of $y = y_o$ the servomechanism does make 'hunting' actions. These can be obliterated by suitable design which relies on the fact that x is a 'continuous' variable. Given continuity the distinction between knowledge of results and direct information is tenuous. But it becomes important when, as at $x = x_{Max}$ there are discontinuities and in the present discussion discontinuity is the rule.

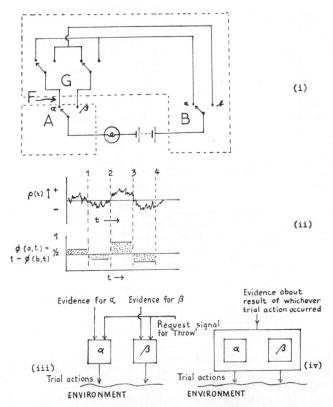

Fig. 14 (i). Dotted lines enclose *A*, an 'on, off' controller and *B*, its 'on, off' environment with characteristics determined by *G*. *F* is a channel coupling *B* to *A*.

Fig. 14 (ii). Hypothetical sequences of signals and evidence.

Fig. 14 (iii). A trial making controller.

Fig. 14 (iv). Autonomous trial making controller.

An *imperfectly* informed controller interacts with an environment enclosed in a black box (as in Chapter 2).

(i). In the place of complete information along *F*, the imperfectly informed controller may only receive a signal $\rho(t)$ as in

Figure 14 (ii), which provides evidence $\phi\,(a,\ t)$, $\phi\,(b,t)$, about the states of the environment, according to the convention that the more positive the average value of $\rho\,(t)$ in the interval $\varDelta t$ preceeding this instant, the more likely is $B = a$ (and the higher $\phi\,(a,t)$) the more negative $\rho(t)$ the more likely is $B = b$ (and the higher $\phi\,(b,t)$). With two mutually exclusive and exhaustive states, one or the other must be the case so $\phi\,(a,t) + \phi\,b,t) = 1$. Obviously if $\phi\,(a,t) = \phi\,(b,t) = 0\cdot5$, no information is conveyed.

(ii). The knowledge of results data may be disconnected or mutilated.

Given either impairment i or ii, completely accurate matching is impossible and we must consider statistical rather than determinate matching between A and B. Statistical matching can maximize the pay-off *on average*, i.e. illuminate the lamp as often as possible.

To illustrate the idea consider the biased dice thrower in Figure 14 (iii). It can throw a 'two-sided' dice each $\varDelta t$, the outcome determining either $A = \alpha$, or $A = \beta$. If the bias is uniform the dice thrower will produce a sequence in which αs and βs are equiprobable. Now this sequence *is matched* to an environment wherein $p\,(a) = p\,(b) = 0\cdot5$ (using the letter p as in Chapter 3, for the actual value of an a priori probability, which depends upon some physical constraint in the environment). Obviously $p\,(a) + p\,(b) = 1$. Suppose we happened to *know* that $p\,(a) = 0\cdot8$ and $p\,(b) = 0\cdot2$ (which is a rudimentary statistical *model* of the environment). The activity of the dice thrower can be matched by adjusting the bias so that the probability of $\alpha = p\,(a) = 0\cdot8$ and of $\beta = p\,(b) = 0\cdot2$. In other words, by building in our 'statistical model'. There are two significant consequences.

(i). If the dice thrower forms part of a controller a matched statistical bias will, by itself, yield an average pay-off better than the pay-off from unbiased chance activity. (The best behaviour if there are *no* sequential dependencies, is to choose α always.)

(ii). The bias can set up a state of 'anticipation' in the controller which combined with otherwise inadequate evidence $\phi\,(a,t)$, $\phi\,(b,t)$ leads to the best action on a *particular occasion t*.

We shall examine a breed of controllers (conditional probability machines and Markovian predictors) that *build up* a statistical model on their own account, on the assumption that the behaviour of their environment is Markovian. They are of increasing practical importance.

Whilst, in some applications, the control system may be a procedure (like quality control of a product) carried out in an office, in others it is a physical device. For the present purpose it is more convenient to think of physical machinery – and (keeping the other connotation in mind) we shall develop the controller from our biased dice thrower. There are two kinds of Markovian controller, namely, 'Predictive' and 'Imitative' or, equally well, 'inert' and 'active'.

Predictive Controllers

The signal $\rho(t)$ may indicate, for example, the expected position of a ship with reference to a harbour, or the expected number of defective items in a batch*. The controller must issue an instruction α or β (helm up or down, reject or accept), whenever, but no more often than each Δt, it is called for by some external request signal. The predictive controller is thus a recipient that derives evidence from $\rho(t)$ to form an *optimum* estimate of the state of its environment. In a more elaborate version it learns to recognize a given state of affairs. Only *after* this has been done, the decision rule is invoked to determine α or β. If an instruction is called for each Δt, the best estimate is $\Psi(a, t) = p(a) \cdot \Phi(a, t) \cdot C(t)$ and $\Psi(b, t) = p(b) \cdot \Phi(b, t) \cdot C(t)$, where $C(t)$ is a constant derived from the condition that $\Psi(a, t) + \Psi(b, t) = 1$. In ignorance of the environment (ship position, number of defective items) this is usually not much help, but given *several*, say m intervals Δt, in which to issue an instruction a controller with a 'memory' register can accumulate evidence. Starting at $t = 0$, and (assuming complete ignorance) with $p(a) = p(b)$:

$\Psi(a, 0) = p(a)$ [we need not write $\Psi(b, 0)$ since $\Psi(b, t) = 1 - \Psi(a, t]$ $\Psi(a, 1) = p(a) \cdot \Phi(a, 1) \cdot C(1) \ldots \Psi(a, m) = p(a) \cdot \Phi(a, 1) \cdot \Phi(a, 2) \ldots \Phi(a, m) \cdot C(m)$

and, as m is increased, either $\Psi(a, m)$ or $\Psi(b, m)$ will approach 1 and the other will approach 0. The stationary values $\Psi(i, m)$ are no more nor less than time averages $\eta(i, t)$ of Chapter 3.

Referring to our decision rule, $A = \alpha$ if $B = a$, $A = \beta$ if

---

* A signal resolved into evidence in favour of one of two possible positions or batch numbers is, of course, absurd. Commonly we are concerned with distribution functions. But the simple case is illustrative.

$B = b$, action (or instruction) α should be biased favourably to an extent $\Psi(a, m)$ and action (or instruction) β to an extent $\Psi(b, m)$. Thus, at $t = m$, these values are applied as a bias to the dice thrower, Figure 2 (ii), which, on receiving a request signal, determines either α or β. For the next set of intervals, beginning at $t = m + 1$, the a priori probabilities $p(a)$, $p(b)$ are replaced by the best estimates, $\Psi(a, m)$, $\Psi(b, m)$ and the predictive controller embarks upon a further cycle. There is just one complication, which is concealed by the oversimplified picture. Normally there are many possible actions, entries and outcomes, and the pay-off matrix contains numerical entries, not just 'on' and 'off'. In particular, some of the outcomes (ship on the rocks, best batch rejected) will be very undesirable, and associated with large negative numbers. Hence the controller takes these values θ_{ij}, $i = a$ or b, $j = \alpha$ or β into account as a further bias upon the dice-throwing process. It 'decides' according to the *consequences* of being wrong or right as well as the evidence that it *is* wrong or right.

The Conditional Probability Machines

Much of the pioneer work upon conditional probability machines is due to Uttley[40], who used them to model certain aspects of nervous activity. He considers an idealized sensory input – binary variables A, B, ... indicating the presence or absence of distinct attributes. States of the environment are represented in a categorizing hierarchy – the lowest level signifying mere occurrence of the sensed properties A, B, ..., the next level signifying the joint occurrence of the properties (event categories such as AB), and so on for higher levels. The hierarchy is realized by electrical units, corresponding with these categories and responding when the events occur, (thus, the A unit responds when A is present and the AB unit when A and B occur jointly). In a conditional probability machine there are registers which compute for each event the average number of occasions upon which it has occurred, thus, over an interval, and assuming a stationary environment the A register will compute η_A and the AB register η_{AB} and these values will approximate the statistical constraints p_A and p_{AB}). The machine is given a rule of inference which entails conditional probability. Let ξ be a constant which, in practice, is about $\frac{1}{2}$.

The machine computes ratios in the form $\dfrac{\eta_{AB}}{\eta_A}$ such that the index of the numerator term is an event category which logically includes the index of the denominator term. If, at a given instant, A occurs and if the ratio $\frac{\eta_{AB}}{\eta_A} > \xi$ then the machine infers the occurrence also of B.

If the machine were perfectly informed (and if the environment were stationary and it functioned successfully) then (after an interval needed to accumulate averages) the inference B implies that the B unit is stimulated. But it is more plausible to suppose that the machine is imperfectly informed – that the stimuli which actuate the first level units are 'evidence' Φ (A), Φ (B), . . . which is sometimes absent even when A and B are present. In this case inference will supplement the inadequate 'evidence'. After learning, the machine infers B, given A, even though – on some particular occasion – the evidence for B is absent.

The machines are much more elaborate and comprehensive than I have suggested, and Uttley's original papers[40][41] should be consulted. I shall conclude this woefully inadequate account with a point he makes in one of these, namely, that if the relation of 'inclusion' is replaced by 'temporal precedence', i.e. if there are delay elements that categorize events A before B, A temporally coincident with B' and 'A after B', then the machine is a predictor and its 'inferences' are predictions which may lead, through a decision rule, to actions.

Imitative Controllers

Imitative controllers come into their own when *no* signal ρ (t) is available although the knowledge of results data is intact (the term 'imitative' is due to MacKay[42], who examines the system in detail). Since the controller has no direct evidence of the state of its environment, it cannot 'learn to recognize' like the predictive devices. Instead the machine 'prods' its environment by an autonomous trial making behaviour. Then it learns which forms of behaviour lead to the best results. In the case we are considering the machine *learns to imitate*.

Referring to Figure 14 (iv) the dice thrower, in an imitative controller, acts continually and autonomously, i.e., *trial actions* α, β, are made regardless of any external excitation. Initially the actions α and β may be tried equiprobably (this is a good strategy – if we do not know what should be done). Some trial activities will make the lamp light. Now, given a 'memory' and given that the environment is a Markovian system, a controller can derive time average estimates η, as in Chapter 3, or conditional probabilities, like $\eta_{aa}=$'The estimated probability, given α at t that the lamp will light, given α at $t + 1$', or $\eta_{a\beta}=$ 'The estimated probability, given α at t, that the lamp will light, given β at $t + 1$. These estimates converge over a long enough sampling interval (*see* Chapter 3) to stationary values lying arbitrarily near p_{aa}, $p_{a\beta}$, $p_{\beta a}$, $p_{\beta\beta}$ and form a transition probability matrix P. Whilst sampling is in progress, it is hard to say what the controller will do, but assuming that $\eta_{ij} \approx p_{ij}$ have been built up in its memory the action is already familiar. Let $J(t) - 1, 0$, if $A = \alpha$ at t, and $J(t) = 0$, 1, if $A=\beta$ at t, (the nomenclature is from Chapter 3). $J(t)$ operates upon P to form a probability distribution $p(t + 1) = p_a(t + 1), p_\beta$ $(t + 1)$, which, since $J(t)$ is binary, is one or other row of P. As indicated in Figure 14 (iv) $p_a(t + 1)$ and $p_\beta(t + 1)$ are used to bias the dice thrower at $t + 1$, as a result of which either α or β is selected and $J(t + 1)$ determined. Hence, P is a statistical model and the equilibrial behaviour given is a statistical decision rule*. If α followed by α tends to light the lamp, then α will tend to follow α, if α followed by β does the trick, then β will tend to follow α. We shall later discuss systems able to 'learn' much longer matching sequences, with no more elaborate knowledge of results, for in principle, an arbitrary degree of matching can be achieved, given long enough to time average. Hence, no $\rho(t)$, no evidence $\Phi(a, t)$, $\Phi(b, t)$ is *necessary* although *if* it is available it can be used as a bias imposed upon the 'state of anticipation' of the dice thrower and less 'learning' will be needed to achieve a given accuracy of matching.

In principle, an imitative controller can deal with a non-stationary environment if there are 'metastable' stationary states. Suppose a transition probability matrix P_1 has been 'learned', then the devil G, in Figure 14 (ii) turns his switch. The controller can perfectly well 'unlearn' P_1 and 'learn' the matrix P_2 needed to deal with this different environment, providing the switch is not turned

---

* This seems to, but in reality does not, disobey the rule that amount of control depends upon the information available to the controller. First, the whole process depends upon the information that the environment is stationary. Secondly, time is taken for learning and the information obtained over this time, adds up to the necessary amount.

too often. Further, given a large memory capacity the controller need not unlearn all about P_1, so if the environment returns to its previous condition P_1 is relearned more rapidly.

As described, only two values of knowledge of results signal are distinguished, but it is not difficult to conceive a multi valued knowledge of results signal (something like 'that was good, that was better") and its magnitude can perfectly well determine how much 'learning' occurs. For obvious reasons this is often called a 'reward' or 'reinforcement' variable. But the controller is not "sure about" the consequences of a trial action, *before* the action is selected. The system does not include a recorded pay-off matrix. *This*, like the 'model' and the decision rule must be 'learned'.

The Adaptive Control System

We have already introduced the idea of control systems which adapt the decision rule in order to achieve stability in a given environment. If any kind of stability will do, the system is called 'ultrastable', which is Ashby's term; if a more specific objective is needed; an adaptive controller. There are two applications. In one the environment is unknown but stationary, when the adaptive controller is used to perform experiments which *could* have been done by its designer, to build a model and to determine an optimum decision rule. In the other, the environment is non-stationary and the controller *must* continually relearn about it. Hence, the imitative controller, learning $P_1, P_2, \ldots$ is adaptive.

As in Chapter 3 we can always view 'learning' as a selective operation and, to start with, this is more illuminating for the logic of an adaptive controller entails an hierarchy *because of which* selective operations can be 'amplified'. To illustrate the point, imagine a busy executive (who acts as an overall controller in the hierarchy) disturbed by m callers. Each hour, to achieve stability and get on with his work, he engages a receptionist (who acts as a sub controller), selected from a set of M possibilities, variety $\text{Log}_2 \cdot M$, perhaps, after several trials. The receptionist who keeps the job is able to perform the selective operation of prevaricating with callers so that, for example, the one who is welcome each hour is accepted, and the $m-1$ are rejected. Her selective operation has a variety $\text{Log}_2 \cdot^m$ per hour. Maybe she lasts 100 hours. The executive has thus gained $100.\text{Log}_2 \cdot^m$ units of selective activity for a mere $\text{Log.}_2 \cdot M$ units, and commonly $m \gg M$. The trick is, he made his selection from the right kind of things – receptionists – which happened to be available. The executive (overall controller) need not know how the receptionists (sub controllers at a lower level in the hierarchy) interact with the environment of callers – he only needs to evaluate the result. In a very real sense, which gives substance to the idea of a 'level', the interaction of sub controllers takes place in an object language (talking about callers), whilst the overall controller has a meta-language (talking about receptionists). There can, of course, be any number of levels.

If we describe the control system as something which 'learns', there are several equivalent pictures. In the first, the M receptionists are replaced by a single one, who does all of the learning guided by a reward variable θ – approval or disapproval meted out by the executive who merely comments upon her behavioural adaptations. In the next picture, the executive does all the learning. He issues instructions (from Chapter 3 we can think of these

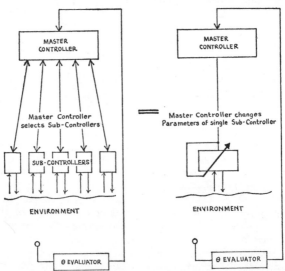

Fig. 15 (i). Equivalent views of an adaptive controller.

changing transition probabilities that govern her behaviour) and learns what instructions induce a fruitful attitude. This, in an industrial system is the method of changing parameters in a sub-controller. Finally, learning may be distributed throughout the system. The hierarchy still has a real logical status, but no physical location *See* Figure 15 (i).

Fig. 15 (ii). Automated factory (see below for key)

Adaptive Controllers in Industry

The recently automated candy factory in Figure 15 (ii) illustrates an industrial application of adaptive control. An indication of successful activity – a reward variable θ, is derived from one of two sources (only one at once) namely – (Mode I) An output meter (1) which measures quality and quantity of candy (according to a predetermined criterion), or (Mode II) a manager (2) who develops a preference for certain states of the plant upon a diversity of evidence, sampling the candy, watching his material bills, and altercating with customers who object to the sweetmeat.

In either case, values of θ are conveyed to a clerk (3). The engineer (4) (having the status of overall controller) knows that the factory can be run by some possibly changing controller, because a limited number of taps used to be turned and a limited number of measures used to be made by men (5) before the place was automated. But the men (5) are disgruntled and will not disclose their arts. So (4) has to experiment by changing the parameters of a versatile sub-controller (which is equivalent to selecting different sub-controllers from a box) (6). For each setting of the parameters (7), the clerk records a value of θ in a table (8) and these records are averaged and guide the engineer who wishes to maximize the average value of θ. Finally (9) and (10) represent the imperfections which disturb any real control system. Actually (8) can take two different forms. If the θ values are recorded conditional upon an independently recognized state of the plant and a particular setting of the parameters, it is a payoff matrix. If the θ values are simply entered under headings 'parameter value' it is a distribution of θ in the phase space of the sub controller. For brevity we shall examine only the second of these alternatives. Hence we are dealing with contours of θ such as those in Figure 16 which could be arrived at by diligent experimenting.

We can, of course, replace the clerk by a 'memory' register and the engineer in Figure 15 (ii) by a computing machine. The problem of control is then a matter of 'How does the machine maximize θ?' and, 'how much experimenting and learning does it have to do?'.

In practice, the controller cannot make each possible trial adjustment of the parameter values and the number needed to sense the θ layout is greatly reduced if there is continuity in the phase space. If so, values of θ lying between a pair of known values can be confidently interpolated. The point is argued by Andrew[43], Box[44], Gabor[46], George[45], and others. It expresses a more widely applicable fact examined in detail by Ashby, that if there is regularity – as a special case, continuity – in the environment the control system will be partitionable into subsystems and 'amplification' of the selective activity is possible. If we confine our attention to Mode (I) some sort of continuity exists – further, choice of a sufficient number of parameters in the initial

(i)　　　　　　(ii)　　　　　　(iii)

PLATE III.
(i) Thread growing
(ii) Developed thread 'breaks'
(iii) Regeneration begins
(iv) Regeneration completed

(*See pages 105-108*)

(iv)

CHEMICAL
COMPUTERS

A and B. Unconstrained systems of unstable threads
using different media. In B
silver, and in A tin threads in
an alcoholic medium. The
thick object is the sensory
electrode

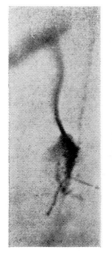

(A)　　　　　　(B)

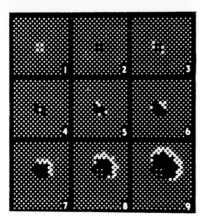

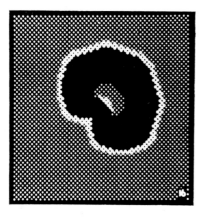

PLATE IV. Activity surge in 2-dimensional cell array of neurone-like units, simulated on a computer by R. L. Beurle

1. Four cells, shown as large white dots, have been activated by an external agency

2. These cells have ceased activity after scattering excitation among their neighbours. This excitation is insufficient to cause spontaneous activity of any further cells. The fact that the four are temporarily out of action is indicated by the absence of the white dots

3. Four more cells are activated by external means

4. The combined excitation has finally resulted in spontaneous activation of a single cell

5. Four further cells are artificially activated. This has really started something

6. Five cells have been spontaneously activated

In periods 7–9 the activity spreads rapidly outwards. From period 8 onwards the cells activated earlier begin to recover their sensitivities. The activity continues to travel outwards, and, at the same time, the cells which were originally active during the first cycle become sensitive again. The process continues as shown in period 16. The last picture conveys some idea of the elaborate forms of activity which are soon induced.

Reproduced by courtesy of R. L. Beurle and the Journal of the Institute of Electrical Engineers design will nearly always reduce a many humped distribution like Figure 16 (i) to a single hump like Figure 16 (ii).

Given the single peak it is not hard to see how the overall controller should maximize θ. It must make trial adjustments and choose whichever of these gives the greatest positive increment of θ, continuing until the increment of θ resulting from a

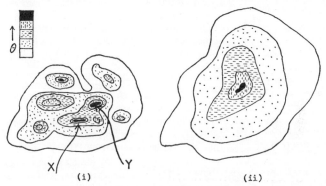

Fig. 16 (i). Multiple maxima in θ contour on phase space with control parameters as co-ordinates.

Fig. 16 (ii). Single maximum in θ contours on phase space with control parameters as co-ordinates

trial becomes either 0 or negative. Overall controllers of this kind are often called 'Hill climbers' or optimizers. Because the controller is informed that there is only one peak it needs only enough 'memory capacity' to retain the results of its immediate trials (a bit more for efficiency or if the environment is non-stationary when it has to learn the location of the different single peaks associated with each metastable state). But if (on grounds of economy) several peaks are tolerated, the 'Hill climber' must have a built-in dislike of apparent success. Thus, using the strategy just described an overall controller might reach X, which is not an optimum peak and it needs to move through a valley into Y, which is. This is more difficult, but if the controller is designed to make occasional trial excursions, even when it has reached θ maximum – a statistical solution is available. The controller will need a larger 'memory capacity' than its simple precursor, in order to retain the hill and valley layout and find its way around.

A number of 'hill climbers' are in use, particularly in the chemical industry. Some like the Westinghouse Optron, and Selfridge's experimental optimizers at Lincoln Laboratories (U.S.A.) are specially built machines, others are computer programmes used to monitor a process. In England, Alex Andrew has rationalized the field of optimum search strategies and his papers[44] should be consulted. In the Russian work Alexei Ivahnenko* has developed a beautiful technique for analysing the behaviour of optimizers within the framework of conventional servomechanism theory.

Adaptive Controllers Able to Deal with a Less Tidy Environment

What about Mode II? In the enlarged system, including customers and suppliers, there is no well defined reference frame, no limited field of enquiry. So Mode II is a trick. I have put the manager there as something unspecified that makes a very large environment intelligible to a computer (or a rational procedure) in terms of a preference ordering θ. I do not think we are yet in a position to replace the manager, though we are well on the way, and we shall discuss some possibilities later. For the moment, notice that an imitative controller is able to go part of the way for, in a certain sense, it can form metalinguistic concepts (for a detailed discussion, see MacKay's paper). Suppose an hierarchy of controllers learning about and trying to *match* each other's behaviour. The lowest level controller imitates its environment, learning that α is more likely than β. The second level learns sequences, α then β, or β then α. The next level learns about and imitates *sequences as a whole*, not α or β as such, and further levels learn about *categories of sequences*. In other words, 'sequences' and 'categories of sequence' become represented by symbols at different levels of discourse and the artifact performs a non-trivial abstraction.

As indicated in Figure 17 (i) any level of the system will learn

* We were fortunate in hearing Professor Ivahnenko's English language lectures, delivered as a guest of the Royal Society. The theme of his work is available in Russian but not, as yet, in English translation [41].

those regularities which enable it, as a whole, to keep in equilibrium with its environment, and receive a reward. Now we need not design the machine to apprehend any particular kind of sequence. For when (speaking mechanically) we say 'it learns' we mean that the elementary subsystems within one of the imitative units have become more closely coupled. True, given some idea of what should happen, it is better to build the artifact on a plan, for example, an hierarchy, but we *can* build it as a bag full of elementary subsystems. In this case, a structure such as an 'hierarchy' occurs *as a result of* the learning process.

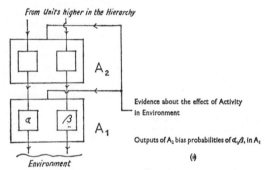

Fig. 17 (i). An heirarchy of trial making controllers.

A Real-Life Artifact

Although developed independently, an automaton of my own called Eucrates, embodies a number of these ideas. Plate I. It is a collection of two kinds of element, namely, 'motor' elements and 'memory' elements, which can be connected in various ways. The name Eucrates relates to a series of special-purpose computers, the first of which was demonstrated in 1955. The illustration shows an apparatus designed by C. E. G. Bailey, T. R. McKinnon Wood and myself and, whilst chiefly intended to simulate the behaviour of a trainee it is applicable also to industrial control.

A motor element in Eucrates is functionally analogous to one of the 'artificial neurones' used by other workers in this field (that is, an electrical circuit or other artifact, which imitates certain carefully specified features of a real neurone but, except in this restricted sense, is not intended as a 'neurone model').

If the input to a motor element exceeds a 'threshold' the element emits an impulse of fixed amplitude and duration. After this the 'threshold' is automatically elevated and no further impulse can be emitted – 'absolute refractory period' is the analogous neurological term. Whilst the threshold returns to its normal value the motor element is more than ordinarily difficult to stimulate relative refractory period), and lacking stimulation, the threshold decreases exponentially to a level at which chance fluctuations will

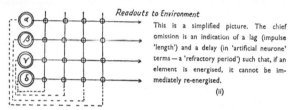

Readouts to Environment

This is a simplified picture. The chief omission is an indication of a lag (impulse 'length') and a delay (in 'artificial neurone' terms — a 'refractory period') such that, if an element is energised, it cannot be immediately re-energised.

(ii)

Fig. 17 (ii). An imitative unit, made up of single action autonomous elements (equivalently 'artificial neurones'), performs trials upon its environment and also interrogates an internal 'memory'. (Each 'memory' register is represented by a small circle at a line intersection). Interrogation elicits the quantities σ stored by a row of these registers, for example, if β makes a trial (emits an impulse) $\sigma_{\beta\alpha}$, $\sigma_{\beta\beta}$, $\sigma_{\beta\gamma}$, $\sigma_{\beta\delta}$, pass by dotted lines to bias further activity. Stored quantities σ commonly depend upon a reward θ (that depends, in turn, upon effect of previous trials).

excite the element (autonomous activity). Groups of elements may have their thresholds linked together by mutual inhibitory connection so that only one can emit an impulse at once. Another interpretation is that each element in the group is competing for a restricted supply of the energy needed to emit an impulse and only one can succeed at once. In either case such a group of motor elements is a basic 'imitative unit'.

'Memory' elements associate the ouput impulses of motor elements with the inputs of others, or connect motor elements to the 'environment'. The 'memory' elements attached to a motor element are analogous to the synaptic connections of a neurone. In Figure 17 (ii) four motor elements are freely interconnectable Suppose, at t, element β emits an impulse, row β of the array is selected. $\alpha\beta$, γ, δ, receive inputs $\sigma_{\beta\alpha}(t)$, $\sigma_{\beta\beta}(t)$, $\sigma_{\beta\gamma}(t)$, $\sigma_{\beta\delta}(t)$, from this row of memory elements. Since $\alpha\beta\gamma\delta$ are grouped, they act as an imitative unit biased by this row. The contribution made by α, for example, given the trial action (output impulse) β at t, is $\sigma_{\beta\alpha}(t)$, hence $\sigma_{\beta\alpha}(t)$ determines the interconnection of these two motor elements. If $\sigma_{\beta\alpha} = 0$, β exerts no effect upon α. If the σ_{ij} of the memory elements are fixed we can regard the array as a transition probability matrix P and proceed as before. In general, however, the σ values change leading to a sequence $P_1, P_2, \ldots$ Thus, in one programme we start off with each σ_{ij} at a small positive value and each σ_{ij} is decreased by a small amount each instant Δt. (This is an inbuilt tendency for connections to decay.) Now suppose α at t, and β at $t + 1$. The one memory element,

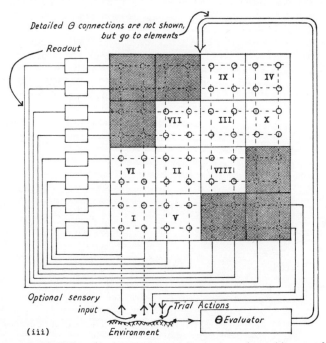

Fig. 17 (iii). Heirarchical arrangement of imitative units and 'memory' registers

lying at the intersection of row α and column β, has its contents increased by an increment proportional to $\theta\,(t+1)\,-\rho_{\alpha\beta}\,(t+1)$ where $\theta\,(t+1)$ is the value at $t+1$ of an external reward variable.

Now it is obvious that various modes of activity and various forms of interaction will build up in the network. The suggested programme implies that those modes of activity which are associated with high values of $\theta\,(t)$ will persist and develop for connections σ_{ij} survive if and only if they are built up faster than the tendency to decay. If, as in Figure 17 (iii). $\theta\,(t)$ is a function of an environment coupled to some of the motor elements (the sensory connections are optional) the simulator learns by trial and reward. Notice that only some of the elements are coupled. If all except the unshaded memory elements were omitted it would be true to say that segment I related environment to environment, segment II internal activity at the first level of an hierarchy to itself, V environment to internal activity, VI internal activity to environment. Segment III defines a higher level in the hierarchy – a part of the network learning about activity in II, and segment IV another level (learning about III) whilst VII, VIII, IX, X couple the different levels. But this structure need not be built into the simulator. It can arise, as an optimum adaptation to the environment by natural selection. Of all the connections which may occur only those which mediate a favourable behaviour can survive.

5

Biological Controllers

At the level of systems, there is no difference between biological and mechanical control. But sometimes the biological controller, as well as the control system, has a ready mechanical analogue. When a limb is moved from position Y_1 to another, Y_2, the muscular contraction depends upon the frequency of nerve impulses arriving at the muscular end plates. Stretch receptors in the muscle signal the degree of contraction along 'proprioceptive' fibres and this feedback to various parts of the brain which are concerned specifically inhibits motor activity and stabilizes the motion. The whole process is monitored by a further, often visual, feedback which conveys a difference signal $Y_2 - Y_1$ which is 0 when the act is completed. So limb movement does involve a two-loop positional servomechanism. Nerve trunks are communication channels carrying impulse frequency modulated signals. If they are cut the servomechanism misbehaves in a predictable fashion. True, fibres in a nerve trunk may regenerate, or alternative pathways may be utilized. But, for practical purposes, the process of repair and adaptation is separate from the everyday functioning. Now this degree of correspondence is exceptional. It does not alter the identity between control systems to point out that most biological controllers are quite unmechanical. Often it is impossible to say. 'that is the controller', or, 'that is the input'. But in biology we must be more than ordinarily careful to think of systems, not things.

Let us briefly review some characteristics of biological control.

1. *Survival.* Consider a biological unit, the single cell. It is an engine such that a system called the 'organism', in this case 'the cell', shall survive in a physical assembly that determines the environment of this system. Unlike mechanical engines neither

energy nor matter are conserved. A degradative tendency, acting to make the system and its environment uniform, is countered by the continual synthesis of constituents according to a largely inherited pattern-embedded in the state of some elaborate, protein bound, nucleic acid molecules, called genes. These control the synthesis of enzymes, protein molecules that act as biological catalysts, which are distributed about the cell and which interact together to control the synthesis of further enzymes and structural materials. Even in this crude picture, two physical distinctions are entailed if the system is partitioned into subsystems; first, spatial distribution, for the nucleic acids are chiefly in the nucleus of the cell, the enzymes are disposed on various reaction surfaces; then chemical specificity, in the sense that enzymes catalyze only certain reactions and combine to form orderly reaction cycles (tricarboxylic acid system, or the A.T.P., A.D.P., phosphorylation, system). Conveniently both spatial distribution and functional specificity are regarded as the consequence of a single process called 'Differentiation'. Hence any coupling between differentiated subsystems tends to involve several physical modalities.

Now, a cell without its nucleus continues to metabolize, but soon falls apart. Equally, the genes cannot replicate without a cell (further, there is evidence that enzyme synthesis is governed by interaction between the genes and the state of the cell, rather than governed by the genes alone). So it occurs that when we speak of an organism, rather than the chemicals it is made from, we do not mean something *described by* a control system. An organism *is a control system* with its own survival as its objective. The basic homeostasis is to preserve itself as an individual.

But in the real world co-operation aids survival, and the pattern we have sketched for a single cell is repeated. There are multicellular organisms, where cells communicate in many ways, where groups of cells differentiate into specialized tissues, and the immediate environment of any one is the community made up of its neighbours, and organisms, in turn, form communities in the social sense.

2. *Adaptation.* To survive in changeful surroundings an organism must be an adaptive control system – or, in this context, an 'ultrastable' system. The most flexible adaptation is learning. The least flexible occurs in evolution, as in the develop-

ment of multicellular creatures. In between, animals are designed to alternate behavioural stereotypes according to the state of their environment. Thus, a hedgehog hibernates in winter.

3. The overall homeostatis, preserving the organism, can be expressed as the conjoint action of many homeostatic systems, each preserving a structure or condition needed for the functioning of the others. Thus, there are systems that regulate body temperature and hydration, and if we enumerate the rest we shall describe the organization of the body. But some care is needed for there is no unique partitioning and few physical structures have an unambiguous function (the limb movement servo is exceptional). The mechanism of breathing, for example, maintains several homeostatic equilibria, depending upon how you look at it (this mechanism will be examined in detail). Conversely, many mechanisms co-operate to maintain one equilibrium. The blood sugar level is the classical case, though it is true of almost any equilibrium state. The enormous stability of an organism is largely due to these complex many-to-many relations between structure and function. McCulloch calls the property a 'redundancy of mechanism' or[48] referring to brains, where these comments apply equally to data processing 'redundancy of computation'. We can, of course, describe any control system as a decision maker, but it occurs that in a system of this kind we cannot say where a decision is made. At one moment A will be dominant, at the next moment B (where A and B are any two subsystems). This further property is called 'redundancy of potential command'.[49] Because of it we must be careful about hierarchies.

There are plenty of them, as in any adaptive control system. The mammalian brain is a somewhat stratified affair, with the cortex commonly dominating the behaviour of substructures which used to be dominant at an earlier stage in our evolution. But, given mescalin, or hashish, or simple pleasure or pain, the order of things is reversed. People exhibit a 'thalamic' behaviour (meaning, quite simply, that in these conditions a particular subsystem, the thalamus, assumes dominance). Again, where is it decided that the heart shall beat? Amongst other possibilities the heart is controlled by the autonomic nervous system and by a pacemaker' in its auricle. Both are sensitive to various chemical and mechanical quantities. These, and the state of the heart, determine which control system is dominant. You cannot, in fact, avoid the problem by saying that autonomic control is mostly concerned with rate, rather than the actual beat, even though this is true. The hierarchies of a biological control system are *not* like those organization charts that purport to delegate function and responsibility to personnel.

4. We have defined an organism as a control system and posed the possibility of partitioning it into subsystems. The extent of the physical mechanism associated with each might be determined by delineating the communication pathways that mediate the control. This is not so easy as it sounds, for in a multicellular animal there are far more modalities of communication than there are in a unicellular and we noted several in that case. What are these modalities? One of the crudest is chemical concentration. If one cell eats up a metabolite in short supply, then the low local concentration is a 'signal' to a neighbouring cell. Or a cell may excrete a specific material which acts on some but not all adjacent cells. Or the material may stimulate a neighbouring cell to produce the same stuff, this in turn stimulates another, and so on down a chain; this is the commonest modality in plants and amongst the colonial amoebae, and the transmission of a nerve impulse in an animal is a refined form of it. At a more specific and familiar level there are hormones (oestrogens, thyroxin) which act upon particular tissues and often conditional upon a particular state of the tissue. There are hormones that elicit other hormones (the pituitary hormones eliciting the oestrogens). Then we come to orthodox channels, nerves conveying signal impulses down definite paths to release a mediating substance (adrenalin, acetyl choline in the mammal) at an effector or a synapse where the joint activity of several incoming fibres may stimulate another neurone.

Nervous transmission is informationally efficient because signals are 'on', 'off' and because they are conveyed rapidly and to specific destinations, But, on all grounds, nervous systems vary a great deal. In man, the central nervous system and the voluntary musculature is associated with nerves that release acetyl choline. An enzyme, choline esterase, breaks this down very rapidly, hence its effects are local and because of this, the close knit, patterned network found in the brain is effective. By way of contrast sympathetic nerves – one component of the autonomic system, concerned with involuntary actions – release adrenalin which acts diffusely like a hormone though it is eventually broken down by amine oxidase. In terms of connection the optic nerve fibres are mapped in detail; at the other extreme, the network in the gut resembles the primitive arrangement of a tiny pond water animal, the hydra.

Finally, the senses and motor actions are communication channels and we cannot be dogmatic about where they end. The visual difference signal $Y_2 - Y_1$ is easy to demark. But if the environment is another man (in conversation), or an adaptive machine (which we shall discuss later on), where does one control system end and the other begin? That depends upon how and why you are looking at it.

Only one biological control system will be examined in detail, but David K. Stanley Jones[50] has recently discussed a large number of these and a mathematical approach is provided by reference [51].

The Regulation of Breathing

Metabolism in the tissues uses up oxygen which is obtained from the arterial blood and it gives rise to carbon dioxide which is carried away in the venous blood. Ultimately oxygen is taken up from the atmosphere, via the lungs where it oxygenates the blood and carbon dioxide is excreted, via the lungs into the atmosphere. An increasing rate and depth of breathing tends to rid the body of carbon dioxide and make further supplies of oxygen available. So, at one level breathing is a homeostatic system which gives a man sufficient oxygen for his metabolic demands and gets rid of sufficient carbon dioxide to prevent intoxication. The first level of regulation keeps the mixture of gases in the alveoli of the lungs at approximately 17 per cent oxygen, 6 per cent carbon dioxide, even though the oxygen demand changes from its resting value of about 250 m.l. per minute to a maximum of 2,500 m.l. per minute and the carbon dioxide excretion from 200 m.l. per minute up to 2,000 m.l. per minute. The regulation is bound up in a whole chain of systems concerned with transporting oxygen and carbon dioxide.

When oxygen passes through the alveoli and into the blood stream most of it is carried in chemical combination with haemoglobin, a substance which exists only inside the red blood corpuscles. Haemoglobin has two chemical forms, namely, oxygenated haemoglobin (HB) OX, and reduced haemoglobin (HB) RE. These forms exist in equilibrium.

$$\text{Oxygen} + \text{(HB) RE} \rightleftharpoons \text{Acid} + \text{(HB) OX} \dots \dots \text{(i)}$$

Carbon dioxide is also carried in chemical combination, chiefly as bicarbonate ions which exist mostly outside the red corpuscles in the plasma and which, in combination with acid, react to yield carbon dioxide and water.

$$\text{Bicarbonate ion} + \text{Acid} \rightleftharpoons \text{Carbon dioxide} + \text{Water} \quad \text{(ii)}$$

Since the concentration (partial pressure) of oxygen in the lungs is high, reaction (i). tends to yield acid and (HB) OX, and the acid acts through reaction (ii) to release carbon dioxide which diffuses out of the blood into the lung.

On closer scrutiny the haemoglobin molecule itself is an ultrastable control system (its chemical activity and structure are modified as a function of its environment), such that between very wide limits of oxygen concentration (partial pressure) the amount of oxygen carried away from the lungs by a given volume of blood remains constant. The mechanisms of ultrastability occur at a sub-molecular level and act upon the equilibrium between the two forms of haemoglobin; thus increase in either acidity or dissolved carbon dioxide favours the dissociative reaction from left to right in (i).

When the blood corpuscle reaches an active tissue it is placed in an environment where the partial pressure of oxygen is low and that of carbon dioxide, diffusing from the tissue fluid through the capillary wall and into the blood, is high. The red corpuscles contain an enzyme, carbonic anhydrase, which catalyzes the reaction:

$$\text{Carbon dioxide} + \text{Water} \xrightarrow{\text{Carbonic anhydrase in corpuscle}} \text{Bicarbonate ion} + \text{Acid} \dots \text{(iii)}$$

Most of the carbon dioxide is absorbed in this process. The acid (hydrogen ion) is used for reducing the oxygenated haemoglobin, as a result of which oxygen is released to the tissues. Most of the bicarbonate ion passes into the blood plasma where it is neutralized by acid groups on the plasma proteins. Hence the reactions inside a corpuscle placed in oxygen-deficient surroundings are:

Carbon dioxide + Water→Bicarbonate + Acid
(from tissues)   (becomes bound by the
                                                  plasma protein in blood)

(HB) OX + Acid→(HB) RE + Oxygen
                                          (to tissues)

...... (vi)

Now all this depends upon a chain of systems, whereby the blood is kept in equilibrium with metabolic activities and the blood itself, corpuscles, plasma, protein and so on, is maintained intact. As an overall result, however, the acidity and the carbon dioxide partial pressure in the arterial blood act as good indices of overall metabolic stability. These indices chiefly control the rate and depth of breathing. Viewed in this way, breathing is a homeostatic system, which keeps the partial pressure of carbon dioxide in the arterial blood at about 14 m.m. Hg., and the acidity at pH 7·4.

Breathing includes inspiration and expiration of air. Inspiration of air occurs through contraction of muscles which lift the ribs and flatten the diaphragm, which increases the chest volume and sucks air into the lungs.

Expiration of air is ordinarily passive: the structures return to their original shape elastically when the muscles are extended, but the abdominal muscles assist the action when deep or rapid respiration is needed. The muscles are enervated from two groups of neurones, the inspiratory and the expiratory groups, situated in the medulla of the brain. Within the medulla itself appreciable activity amongst the inspiratory neurones will inhibit activity amongst the expiratory neurones and vice versa. Connections ascend in the brain from the inspiratory region to further neurones which delay the nerve impulses and return them after delay to excite the expiratory neurones. Taken together these regions constitute the respiratory area which because of the ascending and descending connections, gives forth a rhythmically modulated train of nerve impulses sufficient to sustain rather crude respiration.

The rhythm is improved, the depth and rate of inspiration modified, by a feedback called the Hering Breuer reflex. Nerve impulses from stretch receptors in the lung are returned to excite the expiratory neurones. Thus inspiration and extension of the stretch receptors beyond a limit leads to expiration.

Whilst either mechanism can produce rhythmic respiration alone, they work jointly in the healthy organism (a so-called 'redundancy of mechanism').

The basic respiratory system is controlled as in Figure 18.

1. By the direct action of carbon dioxide and blood acidity

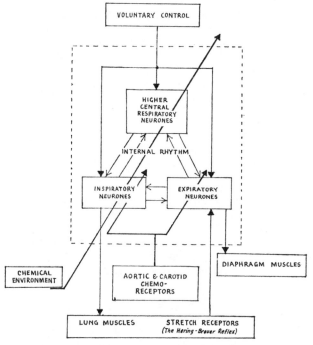

Fig. 18. The respiratory control system

upon the respiratory area. Increase of either variable will increase respiration rate and depth. Individual neurones seem to be unaffected by changes of blood oxygen until it falls to a level at which anoxia and misfunctioning occurs.

2. By nerve impulses from receptors in the aorta and carotid artery bearing on the respiratory neurones. These receptors are somewhat sensitive to carbon dioxide and blood acidity, but

exceptionally sensitive to blood oxygen if its partial pressure falls from the normal value, about 100 m.m. Hg, to below 80 m.m. Hg. Respiratory control *can* be mediated through 1 or 2 alone, but, *normally* the systems co-operate.

3. Voluntary activity can dominate our breathing. A number of variables, such as blood oxygen, nerve impulses from the skin, adrenalin and other hormones, modify the sensitivity of the respiratory neurones and the specific receptors. This action, which is like setting the level of a thermostat provides a special case of ultrastability.

4. Finally, there is interaction with other systems, most noticeably the cardiac control system. There is a deal of interaction in the brain itself and, at a reflex level, the aortic and carotid chemical recepters are closely associated with pressure receptors that mediate several cardiac reflexes and to a limited extent the pathways interact. Finally, the respiratory system depends upon an adequate circulation and chemical equilibrium. Conversely, these depend upon respiration.

The Brain-like Artifact

The brain is the biggest biological control system and the most modelled. First there are simple didactic contrivances such as Grey Walter's 'Tortoise'[52] and Angyan's 'Turtle'[53]. These are animal-like automata, responsive to light, sound and touch stimuli and able to move in various directions. The logical content of either goes into a modest state graph (the possibilities of conditionable reflexes involving a few neurones), but their gambits suggest the behavioural consequences of the theory in a compelling fashion, which is the main object.

Then there are sophisticated models intended *either* as brain artifacts *or* as cognitive automata in their own right (commonly these refer to higher animals). We have encountered two of them already, in the latter capacity, MacKay's imitative controller and Uttley's conditional probability machine. Uttley's machine does embody an explicit hypothesis about the nervous system but its units can be variously interpreted – as neurones, groups of neurones, or unspecified, functional entities.

Next there are brain models, committed to a physiological interpretation. Now these have been advanced in connection with very simple and very elaborate structures. The simple ones are beyond our scope, except to notice that quite a lot is known about the behaviour of neurones individually, their synaptic connections and their behaviour in a ganglion. At the other extreme, is the mammalian cerebral cortex, a laminated mass of richly connected neurones. Oddly enough, we can be more confident about this region than we can about areas of intermediate complexity because it seems almost certain that though the statistical structure and overall layout of the cortex is inherited, the detailed connections are not regular enough to merit attention and are certainly not consistent from brain to brain. Though the details probably *matter* a great deal they cannot readily affect those features of behaviour which are common to all brains. Studies of statistical histology, like Scholl's[54], give plenty of data about the statistical connectivity which *is* present. From this, and information about individual units, it is possible to construct a statistical model* of an arbitary chunk of cortex and test its behaviour against experimentally founded predictions, for example, from Lashley's work[55], that large ablations should exert little obvious effect. Eccles[56] made qualitative proposals some years ago, but R. L. Beurle[57][58] was the first to present a thorough mathematical formulation (*see* Appendix 7).

His model, using 'artificial neurones' is somewhat like the Eucrates system, except that the neuronal parameters are realistic and, in place of a fully connectable network, there is a replica of Scholl's statistical data. In one version, there is a realistically variable connectivity, which simulates synaptic changes.

The model is concerned with properties of neurone aggregates (there is, incidentally, plenty of evidence that neurones cannot, in fact, be considered in functional isolation) and the block of 'imitation cortex' is regarded, for analysis, as a non-homogeneous transmission medium. Activity is manifest as waves of excitation propagated through the medium as shown in Plate IV. If the block is coupled, as in Figure 19, to an environment, it acts as an imitative controller and as no experimental finding is seriously contradicted, it acts as a brain-like controller. I shall baldly state some of its properties.

* If the rules for individual neurones are taken as analogous to the Lagrange equations for the motion of a particle, R. L. Beurle's model of activity in cortical material is analogous to the Gibbs Boltzmann model for a gas.

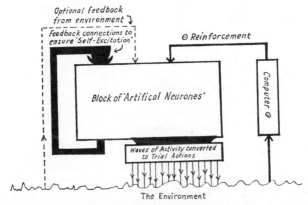

Fig. 19. A self-organizing control system using R. L. Beurle's model

One condition of the model is that not all the elements in a given volume may be excited at once. According to our previous dictum we should interpret this as a stipulation; that there must be competition for the energy needed to maintain activity. Actually, Beurle secures his condition by a special inhibitory feedback but, whatever the details, it is true that transmission of a wave is a competitive process. Also the transmission process entails co-operation (for uncorrelated excitation will be suppressed).

Learning occurs, either through self-excitation of circuits or through plastic changes in connectivity, or both. It is the *form* of a wave that is learned, rather than a set of particular events. The system is able to *generalize* and to build up its *own* criteria of *similarity* between wave forms.

Let a wave λ_1 pass through the medium, inducing plastic changes $\varXi$ which reduce the subsequent impedance of the medium to this particular wave λ_1. Commonly the impedance is also reduced for a set of other waves, say $\lambda_2, \ldots \lambda$. In this sense members of the set $\lambda_1, \lambda_2 \ldots \lambda_m$ are similar with respect to the artifact when they occur upon subsequent occasions.

Two or more waves of excitation may interact with one another giving rise to *progeny*, which is one source of *variation* in the system (another is the autonomous activity of individual neurones). Consider points in the medium so coupled that the artifact is self-exciting and impulses continually recirculate. Since a wave of excitation modifies the structure of the medium in which it is transmitted and the prevailing structure determines the impedance of the medium for a particular form of wave, there is a necessary interaction between structure and activity and vice versa. If a wave λ induces a structure Ξ, and Ξ offers a low impedance to λ, one perpetuates the other and the pair λ, Ξ is a *pattern*. In given conditions a *pattern* may or may not survive but the patterns which do survive are imitated and reproduced.

Finally, recall Figure 19 of the artifact as a controller coupled to an environment and provided by an external arbiter with a reward variable θ. Let us arrange that increase in θ increases the density of elements that can become active (which is the most general kind of 'reward'). Manipulation of θ will lead to natural selection, favouring the reproduction of those patterns which entail an approved behaviour.

We call the artifact, the actual assembly, an 'evolutionary network'.* The network itself cannot be said to evolve (its possible states are always evident). On the other hand, the *active region* in the network which is *the system we refer to as 'learning'* does evolve (an evolutionary network is an assembly which acts as the immediate environment and the material substance of an evolutionary system). It's activity is described by Beurle as wave propagation in a non-linear medium. Peter Greene[65] proposed a method formally comparable to quantum mechanics, for analysing the modes of oscillation. Von Foerster and I have advanced an evolutionary model[66] which lays emphasis upon 'competition' and co-operation'.

Problem Solving

When a control system achieves stability it 'solves the problem' posed by not being stable. To say a controller is a 'problem solver' only when formal logical variables are manipulated and θ is an explicit function of their state seems unduly pedantic. Now we

* Evolutionary networks have been computer simulated (by Beurle[58] Foulkes[60] and using a much more restricted system, Farley and Clark[61]) and realized in a restricted, but logically tractable, way on a special purpose machine (G. D. Willis and his colleagues[62] at Lockheed). By far the most advanced automaton, Plate I(ii), designed for these experiments, has recently been completed by Murray Babcock of the University of Illinois[63].

have seen that some controllers 'learn' how to 'solve problems' and the change of words brings us to the crux of this learning process. For it is not remarkable to find a system has responsive characteristics altered by past events. Given appropriate stimuli this is true of a chunk of iron or a slab of gelatine, certainly of any system with richly coupled subsystems and multiple equilibria. Such systems are conditionable (if a led to α and b to β then, after 'learning', either a or b lead to α) and open, perhaps to operant conditioning (the transition depends upon high valued θ) But a system which 'learns to solve problems' must also learn relations of similarity between them and between the 'sub problems' into which they decompose if only because we *define* problems as instabilities of the environment which *can be* categorized. Operationally, the learning artifact must apply Minsky and Selfridge's 'basic learning heuristic'[64] which reads, 'In a novel situation try methods (parameter adjustments, network organizations) like those which have worked best in similar situations'. (Abstract problem solution does not always have the continuity which is more or less guaranteed in the real world and the necessary parameter adjustments are often less like 'hill climbing' than 'looking for a hill to climb'. In the extreme case of 'true or false' θ contours in the controller's phase space reduce to a flat plain with a single peak at the organisation which solves the problem. θ gives no indication of proximity to a solution. Jack Cowan's work on the possibility of assigning[68] proximity measures (like θ) to problems represented in different systems of logic (Boolean, Lewis, Post) are particularly relevant).

Our evolutionary networks *can* generalize upon their own state, hence, formulate similarities of method, specifying categories of adaptive strategy. Being imitative their image of the world is in terms of possible action. Similarity of method and similarity of situation are not, in this case, distinct. But we must emphasize that the similarity criteria may be unrelated to any that *we* accept and unrelated to the values assumed by θ. They stem from the initial topology of the network and the rules of evolution.

On these and other grounds Minsky and Selfridge[64] doubt the utility of evolutionary networks and approach problem solving from the viewpoint of 'artificial intelligence'. A typical intelligent artifact is the Newell, Shaw and Simon computer[67] programme for learning to prove logical theories. It is not 'automatic', but permissible operations and heuristics (broad suggestions about fruitful procedures, for example; suggestions about what is and what is not similar) are well defined.

Whilst admitting their contention, in the case of formal problem solution, I do not share their pessimism about evolutionary networks.* Often in real life control, a solution is needed but the method of achieving it is irrelevant. The network also comes into its own when we, ourselves, cannot formulate a problem. We see a chaotic world, i.e. an inherently unstable process, and wish for order of any kind. Now *efficient* control does depend upon (in some sense) matching the evolutionary rules of the network to those of the world. I agree that when we have said in *what* sense, the matching process may amount to 'finding a good heuristic', in which case the evolutionary approach and artificial intelligence are complementary.

Recognition and Abstraction of Forms

Receptive controllers need a diversity of evidence and particular fixed instances are inadequate. Rather, we must examine the mechanisms underlying the abstraction of an observer (Chapter 3) Suppose a visual sensory field, a retina of n binary receptive elements (rods, cones). The forms which interest us are, for example, characters 'R', '8' .... Now, although we define the character 'R' ostensibly by pointing to $R \approx$, RR, R^R, Rr – as instances of 'R' neither a finite automaton nor we ourselves register each exemplar, even less the black and white particles that make it up. What we mean by 'R' is something invariant under various groups of transformations of the figure (first pair, rotations, second pair, dilations, third, displacements, and fourth a non-geometrical transform called upper to lower case), in short, a Gestalt. The primary result in recognition was obtained by McCulloch and Pitts[69][70] when they showed that a

---

* But I do not condone a lot of loose talk about 'random networks'. 'Random network' *should* mean a very definite initial structure determined by a random number table, presumably because the initial structure does not affect those features of behaviour that interest us, providing the behaviour is averaged over an ensemble of artifacts (as used by Rapoport, Shimbel, Uttley). But, in literature it *can* mean almost anything. In particular neither R. L. Beurle's model nor mine are random networks. One has the statistical constraints of a brain. The other is fully connectable.

finite automaton – a fixed network of 'artificial neurones' – could extract Gestalten.

Recently Lettvin and Matturana, working in collaboration with McCulloch and Pitts,[71] have discovered a network in the frog performing abstraction up to the level of a conceptual category, a primitive Gestalt. The frog retina is divided into regions, receptive fields, containing many receptors. For each receptive field, networks among the bipolar and ganglionic neurones compute the value of four distinct attributes:

(i) Presence of sharp edge of an object imaged upon the receptors.
(ii) Convexity of dark object.
(iii) Movement of an edge.
(iv) Overall dimming.

These attributes have significance to the frog, for example (ii) is almost perfectly a bug detector (and he eats bugs), whilst (iv) indicates a predator. The frog sees his world in this reference frame, not as patches of black and white.

Fibres from each receptive field travel in the optic nerve to four layers of the colliculus, one attribute to each layer, neighbouring receptive fields to neighbouring segments. The dendrites of deeper cells ramify amongst each layer, hence any one receives, in terms of relative excitation, evidence about the locus of a state point in a four-dimensional attribute space, that characterizes a particular receptive field. The ensemble of possible loci is the frog's universe of discourse, a subset of the ensemble a conceptual category. The frog decides whether his immediate environment is in a given category and takes action accordingly.

The design of attribute filters is a well-developed art (such things as convexity receptors, number of angle receptors, area, overall curliness, are easy), and extends also to less tidy, but more natural percepts (neither a teapot perceptor nor something especially sensitive to blondes is absurd).*[73] But though they

---

* Consider a sensory field, for example, a retina with n light sensitive receptors and a given property, such as squareness. The design of a filter to extract (or detect) this property in retinal images can always be approached by brute force – specify subsets of logical elements in parallel – each subset sensing one square form, then combine their outputs. But the number of elements, about 2^n, is absurd. The frog does the job more efficiently. But he sees bugs, not what *we want* him to see. The group working at the University of Illinois[69] are concerned

may involve internal feedback these are fixed filters. We can use them to imitate frogs, for a frog does not 'learn' to recognize new 'percepts' and there is plenty of evidence, from regeneration experiments, to show that his attribute space is genetically determined. Man, on the other hand, spends most of his days 'learning to recognize'. The dilettante observer of Chapter 2 is the rule of behaviour, the scientist an exception. For a readable account of our odd, changeful and intensely personal attribute space, our cognitive world, see M. L. Johnson Abercrombie's book.[72] But even we have something inbuilt. Some results from Cooper and his associates at Haskins Laboratories, show what happens for hearing. We are born with gene determined filters that select attributes of speech sounds – such as the attribute common to 'bi', 'ba' and 'bu'. In our social environment we learn, not new attributes, but the yen to regard certain values of the attribute as identical (those that utter 'bi' and those that utter 'ba') and to discriminate these sets of values ('bi' and 'ba') as distinct.

Learning to Recognize Forms

When it comes to making cognitive 'pattern recognizers' there is argument over the merits of 'pre-programmed' and 'learning' machines. A wholly inflexible device has little practical value for even printed characters come mutilated or displaced from their reference position. The most stereotyped but still useful machines (I happen to know the Solartron E.R.A.) work at frog level. At the other extreme, Frank Rosenblatt[74] has a particularly malleable network, the 'Perceptron', that can be trained (essentially by operant conditioning) to recognize characters. Facilitated paths in the trained network determine the attribute filters. By compari-

---

with input filters for self-organizing systems which must be able to detect *arbitrarily chosen* attributes. They have tackled the design problem in several ways. One approach has been to reduce the 'size' of the 'artificial neurones' in a network until the network itself becomes a transmission medium described by continuously expressed filter characteristics that depend upon a distribution of connectivity (one worked out case is a curvature detector). Another approach makes use of topological relations between retinal images and particular types of discrete connectivity. One worked out case is a number detector, not a counter, but something which appreciates how many objects without counting them. The realizations of either approach can be transformed into each other.

son with a structured automaton the Perceptron learns slowly. However, this is no real criticism (more cogent criticism is aimed at its limitations as an abstractive device) and the device would come into its own if we did not know exactly how or what to recognize at the outset. It is difficult, for example, to specify a 'defect' in a woven fabric – but a trainer can recognize a defect when it occurs and tell a Perceptron, inspecting the same sample, that it should copy his preferences.

Nearly always we *can tell* the machine something and, surely, we *should tell* it, as part of its programme. But we should not prevent it indulging its own breed of recognition or expect logical nicety amongst the attributes it selects. We do not really recognize signatures in terms of neat geometrical attributes – they 'remind us of faces' or seem more or less 'wiggly' and we must tolerate just as unruly attributes in an automaton.

Nearly always, also, the optimum selection of descriptive attributes will change with experience and an adaptive machine is needed. Oliver Selfridge's form recognition computer programme, 'Pandemonium,' is a happy compromise.[75] It is an hierarchy of sub-routines or computing elements, whimsically called 'demons'. On top is a master-demon which receives inputs from several lower-level cognitive-demons. Each cognitive demon assimilates evidence that the state of the environment has a particular form, i.e. R or 8 and provides an output indicating its degree of conviction. The master-demon decides that one or another state exists by selecting the cognitive-demon with the largest output. The cognitive-demons receive their evidence from sub-demons (analogous to sub-controllers) which we interpret as attribute filters. Now the master-demon and cognitive-demons together are an 'overall controller' and they obtain an evaluation θ upon the 'adequacy' of their performance from an external source. To maximize θ the attribute filters are adjusted (i.e., evidence from the several sub-demons is differently biased) which entails hill-climbing in the phase space of the Pandemonium.

But the initial selection of sub-demons is arbitrary, conceivably stupid, and it may be necessary to discard some unsuccessful sub-demons and acquire new ones. To avoid losing all trace of the previous adjustments fresh sub-demons are constructed by combining the components of the old demons in a different way. Hence the system is evolutionary.

6 Teaching Machines

TEACHING is control over the acquisition of a 'skill' (which after Bartlett, implies conceptual gambits like speaking a language and solving a problem, as well as 'motor skills' such as type-writing or flying an aeroplane). The old idea that repetition writes engrams on to the fallow brain has been discarded (and also, with the possible exception of latent learning, the notion that man resembles a tape recorder). Learning is active and occurs when there is motivation. Teaching entails some effort on the teacher's part. Hence, a 'teaching machine' interacts with a student. Magic lanterns and simulators, that merely present data, do not 'teach'.

The first 'teaching machine' was devised by S. L. Pressey[76] about 1920. Whilst he recognized its instructional role it was chiefly intended as an automatic intelligence tester. The student is presented with questions selected by a programme (a primitive syllabus). He answers by selecting one of several alternative response buttons and is marked right or wrong by comparison with a programmed code (a primitive text-book). If right, the machine presents the next item in the question programme. If wrong, the student is informed and must make another attempt.

Norman Crowder[76] has developed a much more flexible machine. Programmed items are back projected from film strip on to a translucent screen. A typical item is a page of written or diagrammatic material describing a principle. Teaching algebra, for example, it might be one of the principles, like substitution of variables, needed to solve simultaneous equations. Also there are problems embodying the principle and alternative answers. The student selects one of these by pressing buttons, and his response is evaluated. The machine 'decides' the next item according to its evaluation. If 'correct', for example, it presents the next item in the programmed sequence. If in 'error', it selects a sub-programme designed to eliminate whatever misconception is revealed by the particular kind of error.

Skinner has contrived a somewhat different teaching machine.[76] The student composes a response, rather than selecting one from a given set, and he makes his own evaluation against 'correct response' data supplied by the automaton. In addition, Skinnerian programmes are built up in minimal and always comprehensible stages. There are, nowadays, many variations on each of these themes. But, from a cybernetic viewpoint, all such fixed programme teaching machines are 'automatic controllers'. They provide 'knowledge of results' feedback which motivates the student and an unknown, or if the programme is repeated, unlearnable, sequence of items to provide the requisite variety. The underlying assumption is that a best method of teaching exists and this is embodied in the programme and the decision rule that determines the machine behaviour. There is plenty of evidence that teaching machines work passably well. But because of the fixed programme which embodies it, the method can only be best for an average student – for those aspects of behaviour which are stationary when averaged over an ensemble of individuals (by definition, *the student who learns* is non-stationary. What the programmer assumes is an *invariant sequence* of stationary states, that characterizes optimum learning of the skill).

Now this puts the onus for adaptation upon the student. He must accept the probably laudable dogma of the machine – and he does. In contrast, a real life private instructor, although he knows what he wants to achieve, has few preconceptions about how to achieve it – and he continually adapts his teaching method to the changeful quirks of each individual. Like the fixed programme machine he observes the student's response. Unlike it, he changes his decision rule, even his syllabus, and the interaction has the logical status of a conversation, which entails compromise between the participants at each stage. The private instructor is at least an adaptive controller and there is reason to believe that, for some skills, he is more efficient than a fixed programme device.

Adaptive Teachers

In 1952 I became interested in the interaction between men and 'learning' machines, constructed some rather whimsical automata and managed to achieve a stable, in a certain sense, a 'conversational', man/machine relationship. Since 1956 Bailey, McKinnon

Wood and I have applied similar methods to the synthesis of teaching systems which will act as private instructors.[76]

Suppose we have to teach maintenance of a data processing equipment made up of eight units performing logical operations

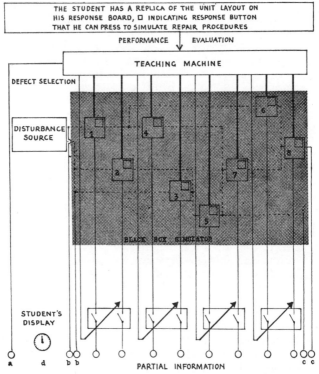

Fig. 20. Structure of an adaptive teaching system used for maintenance training

like 'and', 'or', and that the simulator of Figure 20 is available. In the simplest case, any unit may become defective, but only one at once, and the student is informed, by a signal lamp *a*, whenever there is a defect. In real life he is required to locate and replace the defective unit. On the simulator he selects one of the eight unit positions on the layout panel in front of him, and presses a button to indicate replacement. The student is also provided with the input state (binary variables represented by signal lamps b) and the output state (signal lamps c) of the equipment. This information is available in real life and, again in the simplest case, a short sequence of it, *logically specifies* the defective unit. Hence, a *fully trained* person can select the right unit and repair it immediately. But, before training, the simulated equipment appears as a "black box", and given no further information the student flounders around, trying replacements until one of them puts out the defect lamp. To prevent this hapless guess-work, the simulator can, but need not always, provide 'partial information' about the state of the individual units (allowing the student to 'see inside' the black box), which is not available in real life. Suppose that there are four states of partial information, none, α, β, and γ. Since time is at a premium, we should like the student to deal with defects as rapidly as possible – so he is allowed a maximum time after which he must give up – indicated by a clock d. (In fact, the clock rate, and thus the allowed interval is a further variable, manipulated by the teacher.) Finally, an index of successful performance $\theta(t)$ is computed and displayed on a dial.

It is not too difficult to find a measure $\theta(t)$ with the obviously necessary property that it is minimized by aimless floundering, and/or undue sloth and maximized if the student deals correctly with each defect $i = 1, 2, \ldots 8$, when the defects appear with their real life probabilities. This last stipulation avoids spurious success due to dealing with a few favoured defects. We shall construct a plausible measure. Let each response to each defect i, be compared in an electronic comparator, with a programmed 'text-book' that specifies the correct replacement, given i. Let $\xi_i(t) = 1$, if, and only if, at t, the i-th defect is presented and the correct replacement made, if not, $\xi_i(t) = 0$. Let $R_i(t)$ be inversely proportional to the student's latency upon this occasion. Let p_i be the real life probability of defect i and $\chi i(t)$ its frequency of occurrence at this stage in the teaching process. Then, at an instant $t = t_0$, we define:

$\theta*(t)_0$ = Average over all defects i, average over an interval $t_0 - \tau$, of $\xi_i(t) \cdot R_i(t) \cdot [1 - (p_i - \chi_i(t))^2]$

Of course, $\theta^*(t)$ is one of many possible measures – in particular – it takes no account of information derived from mistaken responses (since we do not know the significance of mistakes) and is descriptive *if and only if a correct response occurs within the allowed interval*. Hence, we *must* introduce partial information in order to ensure that a reasonable number of defects can be dealt with, and that $\theta^*(t)$ *is* descriptive – if for no other reason. But if we do, the job of selecting a replacement is degraded. Success with partial information should count less than success without it. Thus we define a cost of partial information $= \delta$ if there is some partial information, 0 if there is *none* (there are no grounds for supposing that α or β is more valuable than γ, or vice versa). Finally, let $\theta(t_0) = $ Average over i, average over $t_0 - \tau$, of $[\xi_i(t) \cdot R_i(t) \cdot [1 - (p_i - \chi_i(t))^2] - \delta(t)$.

A training routine is a sequence of defects selected together with some state of the partial information, that is, a sequence of problems. An optimum training routine is a sequence of problems, such that the rate of increase in $\theta(t)$ is maximized. Consider first how a machine like Eucrates, programmed as an evolutionary network, learns to select the defects of an optimum routine. As in Figure 20, its output states (a subset of its possible states) are associated with defects, i.e. its trial actions introduce defects into the simulator. $\theta(t)$ is used as a reward variable which selects modes of organization, i.e. systems which behave as required. Now consider the partial information. In practice a separate machine (a sub-controller) is coupled to each defect and the i-th sub-controller is supplied with an individual average $\theta_i(t)$ of $\theta(t)$. States of the i-th sub-controller are related to states of the partial information which is delivered with the i-th 'defect' and it presents or withdraws the partial information to maximize $\theta_i(t)$. This arrangement has been experimentally realized. The system as a whole becomes stable. Haphazard trial making gives place to coherent patterns, *systems* in the network that are reproduced. Soon after this measurable coherence is manifest the student reports a sense of participating in a competition (some say a conversation) with a not dissimilar entity.

Descriptive Model

To make sense of the process we must talk about *systems*. A brain is modified by its history, but, like any other evolutionary network, *it* does not learn. The student who *does* learn is a system developed *in* the brain. When the system as a whole is stable the two subsystems, man and machine, are indistinguishable and the student uses bits of machine like bits of his brain in solving a problem. But this does not mean they are physically meshed together.

The 'conversation' that leads up to this state entails two formally distinct activities:

1. The controller must 'keep the student's attention' which is a special case of 'requisite variety'. The student is a system with given variety of behaviour, say u; that is, he *must* attend to something. u is a measure of the rate at which data of some kind must be processed, or decisions of some kind made, in order that the system shall have the status of a 'student'. Suppose, then, that he does attend to the problem display. The variety of a problem, with reference to the student – for short – its 'difficulty', is the amount of decision making needed to reach a solution (imagine a choice process, whereby uncertainty about a response is reduced until one response is actually made). Now to keep the student's attention the controller must select a sequence of problems which have an average 'difficulty' at least equal to u. Unless it does, the student will daydream. Unfortunately, if it does, there is no *guarantee* that he will not. But, given the matching condition to be cited in 2, $\theta(t)$ is an estimate of overall difficulty and the defect selection tends to satisfy the requisite variety condition.

2. Problems must be matched to the student. At the lowest level, partial information sub-controllers do this job. They give plenty of partial information, making the problems intelligible to start with and then withdraw it (α first, or β first, according to their adaptation) as $\theta_i(t)$, for the i-th sub-controller, becomes greater.

This is not the whole story. Problems are not appreciated as unitary entities, and their sequential ordering is equally part of the matching process. In turn, this depends upon the generalizations built up in the controller. Recall the operational definition of meaning in Appendix 5, namely, the selective function of a message relative to the student, and the notion that messages operate upon the attitude of a recipient. Now, problems act as messages in the required sense, for the act of decision does modify the student's attitude, and 'matching' as used here, means setting up conditions that render messages meaningful, or equivalently, adapting the object language of the discourse to suit the student.

1 is impossible unless 2 is approximately satisfied, for $\theta(t)$ is arbitrary. 2 is obviously impossible without 1. So it all depends upon the student, and however cajoled, there is no guarantee he will attend. But once the 'conversation' has started it has an inherent stability that stems from two-sided adaptation. Student and machine reach a compromise.

What does the student gain by this co-operation (tautologously, a chance to communicate)? The trite reply is an increase in θ, as displayed on his dial – which is a sort of payoff. But, after looking at the way people behave, I believe they aim for the nonnumerical payoff of achieving some desired stable relationship with the machine. The dial is of minor importance. Indeed, in other teaching devices it is omitted.

The obvious criticism; that a real machine cannot have the information capacity of a brain, even in a restricted universe of discourse, is answered by this co-operative process. The system develops not unlike an embryo, by autocatalysis. At the first stage, the presence of the teaching machine gives rise to a system, an organization, which catalyses the appearance of a similar but larger system. This engenders another, which is also catalytic. In a teaching system we require that the sequence of catalytic systems have behaviours that lead to greater proficiency, at the skill concerned.

To summarize; in conversation a controller is aiming:

1. To keep the student's attention. This action is *competitive*, since increasing problem variety at t, tends to defeat the student at t. However, it does induce him to learn and thus gain greater success at $t + 1$.

2. To adapt the object language, which is a largely co-operative affair.

In a skill like fault detection we cannot practically separate 1 and 2. But these functions are separable when there is a well-defined method of stage-by-stage learning.

Add Listing

Trainees learning to work a ten-key add listing machine have to translate chunks of numerical data such as '1278', '253467 (obtained, in real life, from invoices) into rapidly performed sequences of key depressions. At the outset, each chunk poses a realistic problem, and it happens that people learning this skill describe the problem in terms of more or less consistent descriptive attributes.* Some of these are:

(i) Number of items in a chunk of data. (Two attributes.)

(ii) Whether the items entail horizontal runs on the keyboard (given the usual layout '123', '456', '789'), or

(iii) Vertical runs like '147', '258', and '369'.

(iv) Specific constraints such as 'all items selected from the subset 2–8'.

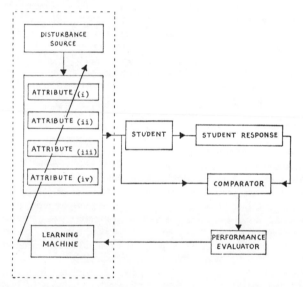

Fig. 21. An adaptive teaching system applicable if the skill entails well-defined perceptual attributes

* The integrity of an attribute depends upon a transitive ordering under the measure function, i.e. whether increasing its value increases the 'difficulty'. Many numerical attributes are deceptive. It is more difficult to deal with six than with three items, more difficult to deal with five than four, but because of the keyboard layout five may be more or less difficult than six. Hence, we use two number of item attributes.

Hence a problem is conceived as something possessing or not possessing these attributes in varying degree and the skill is performed after the manner of an elaborate frog that deals with specified conceptual categories. We use a teaching system of the kind in Figure 21.[77] The controller learns the effect of changing attribute values upon θ (as before, computed from the student's performance). Then, hill climbing in the attribute space, it aims to maximize θ. The mechanical arrangement involves an attribute filter used in reverse. A given state of the controller specifies, for example, that the data presented at this instant shall have four items selected from numerals 2–8, and a horizontal run. The 'dice thrower', which supplies the requisite variety, selects some problem from the specified set. Now, for any state of the controller, Figure 21, is a relabelled version of Figure 6 in Chapter 3. Hence, recalling the discussion, this teaching machine presents the student with a suitably adapted sequence of models of the environment he must eventually deal with.

Card Punching

For most keyboard skills the teaching system can be partitioned into separately adjustable variables with a consequent reduction in controller search time. Card punching of business machine input data cards, is a case in point.[76] Trainees are given exercise lines of twenty-four items of alphabetical or numerical data. This is long enough, under working conditions, to prevent the student learning the entire sequence. For each numerical character the student selects one of twelve keys, for each alphabetic character, a pair, and after training a response time (or latency) of about 0·2 seconds is required. To avoid technical niceties I shall describe a prototype, but SAKI of Plate II is a production machine derived from it. There are two displays. The upper display is a set of four programmed 'exercise lines' and is inserted together with a programmed 'text-book'. Each exercise line is designed to be different. For example, one may have particular sequences of items; one may lack alphabetic items; and so on. The machine selects one exercise line for rehearsal and when it does so an indicator moves from right to left showing which item the student must deal with. The lower 'cue display' is an array of signal lamps arranged as a replica of the keyboard. Initially, as the indicator moves along the exercise line these are illuminated to show, in the case of a numeral, the correct response key position or, in the case of an alphabetic character, the correct response pair.

The machine adjusts four sets of partitioned variables:

1. After each rehearsal, it selects a further exercise line, possibly the same one. The selection depends upon a performance measure, averaged separately for each exercise line. The one with the least valued measure is selected. Hence, the student receives most practice upon the sequence he finds most difficult.

2. The interval allowed for dealing with each item, a pacing variable, is determined by a measure computed and registered in a separate memory device for each item. Let Δt_i be the interval allowed for the i-th item, and T_i the latency. This measure is a weighted average of differences. $\Delta t_i - T_i$ taken for previous occasions when the student made a correct response (an error response subtracts an increment from the measure). Δt_i is the machine's prediction of T_i and with experience Δt_i approaches T_i at a rate determined by the weighting. If we think of a choice process, going on in Δt_i to decide the student's response to the i-th item, reducing Δt_i makes the student respond when he is less certain; for, if he does not respond soon enough, he cannot respond at all.

3. We can think of 'cue information', which is equivalent to 'partial information', assisting the choice process and compensating for a reduction in Δt_i. But its appearance can be delayed until late in the allowed interval or it may be removed altogether. The machine has a tendency to delay the cue information, which builds up at a rate β for each item. This tendency is reversed if the student makes error responses, on this item, or if he does not respond. Notice that when the machine selects an exercise line, it does not merely select a sequence of items but a sequence of *problems* determined by the Δt_i and the cue information delays associated at a given stage with each *item*.

4. The machine adjusts the parameters α and β so as to maximize an average correct response rate $\theta(t)$.

To start with, items are presented slowly at a uniform rate, and together with complete cue information. Each exercise line is presented in turn. This is a period of experimentation when the teaching machine builds up a pattern representing the student's behaviour in its memory registers. As the student becomes proficient the pace is increased and the cue information selectively

D

withdrawn. If, as a result of this adjustment, the student makes an error response, say at the i-th item, or even without error, responds slowly, the process is reversed *for the* i-*th item*, i.e. the machine *increases* Δt_i and brings back the i-th item cue information.

Learning curves for card punching have plateaux corresponding with the mastery of sub skills which entail grouping of data into conceptual categories that are appreciated and responded to as a whole. An experiment, due to Van der Veldt, illustrates the point.[78] Van der Veldt's subjects were presented with a rectangular array of signal lamps, each one named by a nonsense syllable. The experimenter announced a nonsense syllable and the corresponding lamp was illuminated and the subject, viewing the board indirectly, was required to locate the illuminated lamp. At first the subject could only deal with single nonsense syllables. Later he grouped the lamps into sub sets and made a combined movement in response to a word made up of several nonsense syllables. Ultimately, after using this response mode, he was unable to locate a single lamp, evoked by a single syllable, except by reference to the group in which it was included.

The grouping which exists at a given stage is reflected in the distribution of values in the memory registers. The action of the teaching machine encourages the student to increase the size of his group. Ultimately the cue information is withdrawn completely and the pace is maximized.

The system as a whole can reach a stationary state if, and only if, the student is making correct responses at a rate determined by the maximum excursion of the control parameters, and supposed adequate to satisfy the fully trained performance criteria, and if he is doing so for each kind of material.

Aptitude Testing

The usefulness of adaptive systems is not limited to teaching, indeed, they promise to be of greater value in connection with aptitude testing. By definition, a pair of inherently unmeasurable, non-stationary systems, are coupled to produce an inherently measurable stationary system. Of course, it is the set of adapted problems rather than the exercise programme itself which constitutes the test material, but the state of the teaching machine which determines the array of problems, at each instant, can be asserted in terms of electrical potentials. From these we know what changes are needed to produce a stable relationship between student and machine, given a particular exercise programme and a particular student, and there is some evidence to suggest that these stability characteristics are a basis for predicting the student's subsequent performance.

7 The Evolution and Reproduction of Machines

THERE is no mystery about machines that reproduce. From Chapter 3 a machine is a state determined subsystem – the simplest exemplar, a 'Turing machine'. Turing himself considered a further, so-called 'Universal machine' which is the same thing equipped with an indefinitely large memory (an infinite tape with positions for binary digits) and means for 'writing' its state into this 'memory', shifting position, and reading the contents. He showed that a universal machine can adopt any 'writing' behaviour which could have been 'written' by any universal machine, in particular, it can construct a pattern which describes itself. Von Neuman later developed a theory in which the selective operation of 'writing' is replaced by the selection of 'standard' components from a bag. Thereby a universal machine can assemble a pattern of components which is a replica of itself. So reproduction in a logical environment is possible. The trick lies in having a bag of the right components (for a fuller discussion see Beer[11], or Lofgrew[79], or the original papers[26]). The Von Neuman machine and its environment are commonly represented by the states of a computer, but if, as I do, you like a mechanical analogy for the logical prerequisites of reproduction, you should read one of the articles where Penrose[81] supplies it.

A parent machine determines the orderly development of an offspring from components in plentiful supply. If we add to this picture:

(i) A source of variation, and

(ii) A selective or competitive process that acts upon the machines as a whole,

then successive generations may evolve. (i) implies that not all replicas are perfect. To realize (ii) consider an environment wherein some components are scarce. Now suppose that one variant is at an advantage in the competition for scarce components – that it uses them in producing machines of a like kind, and thus inhibits the development of other species. In a Darwinian sense, the variant is better fitted for survival. But, for sensible evolution, we also require that variants which are better fitted have some property in common, that there is a recognizable, evolutionary trend. The trend, of course, is derived from a relation between the machines and their environment. Let us assume an environment such that the best fitted machines have the property of co-operative interaction between their parts (we make our abstract model correspond with our notions of Chapter 5). Then, as Burke points out,[80] a successfully evolving species of machine is likely to construct, and make self-referential 'statements' in an hierarchy of metalanguages. In other words, a member of this species will generalize about its own state and construction. A 'system' developing in one of the evolutionary networks we have already discussed is isomorphic with a member of this species.

Recall; the competitive element is introduced by a commodity (energy, perhaps) needed in order to build up the connectivity to mediate a system and maintain its activity. If there is not sufficient of this commodity, a system does not survive. Further, the surplus of the commodity is determined by a reward variable θ, which depends upon the behaviour of system in the evolutionary network. In these conditions, when the network is used as a controller, it becomes equivalent to say that 'a system aims to maximize θ' and 'a system aims to survive'.

In these conditions, also, a system (say, A) will evolve *because* it encounters a situation which is undecidable in the object language of its interaction with the controlled assembly. Suppose, for example, that A_1 'decides' about unitary entities and that no unitary action will maximize θ. Then A_1 has two alternatives (since the possibility of remaining A_1 indefinitely can always be excluded by adjusting the surplus), namely:

1. To evolve into system A_2, such that the object language of A_2 is a metalanguage in which the situation *is* decidable (perhaps A_2 'decides' about *sequences* of actions, and some sequence does maximize θ), or

2. To come apart, since there is insufficient of the necessary commodity to maintain it.

Of these, 1 is only possible if the existence of A_2 is rewarded in the same way that the existence of A_1 must have been. So the man or computer manipulating θ should, in fact, reward an evolutionary trend A_1, A_2 . . . rather than a particular system. In order to do this, the trend must be recognized, which is much the same as recognising the similarity criteria of Chapter 5. But recall that the 'trend' is initially determined by a relation between A_1 and the environment, i.e. the network structure. So we return to the dilemma of Chapter 5, the issue of what to 'build in'.

However, there is one redeeming feature, which accounts for the 'autocatalytic effect' noted in Chapter 6. Over an interval many systems evolve and the environment of any one system becomes increasingly determined by this population and less by the initial structure.* Now it is possible for an observer to make sense of what goes on – to adopt a good rewarding procedure – providing he 'converses' like the student in a teaching system. But, as a result of this close coupled interaction he fashions the system in his own image.

The Self-Organizing Systems
In Von Foerster's department we studied the competition and co-operation between evolving systems. The population is rarely homogeneous; different species co-exist in dynamic equilibrium. For various reasons it is particularly interesting when a hybrid of several previously distinct species becomes more stable than any one (the hybrid is dubbed 'resonant' by analogy with a resonant molecule, such as benzene, where a hybrid form is more stable than any of the classical descriptors. As with the molecule it is important to realize that the hybrid is something 'novel' and not an admixture of the descriptors). An evolving hybrid is a self-organizing system, as defined in Chapter 3, in terms of its relation to an observer, for an observer must continually change his reference frame to make sense of it.† But, in this context, to

* The species determines its own environment. In natural evolution this is the feature which distinguishes man. The most fitted variant is somebody who is adapted to a man-made environment.

† Notice (i) The system evolves, hence is non-stationary, so an observer must resort to averages μ_{ij} over an ensemble of similar systems. But resonance implies that no single criterion of similarity will be adequate.

(ii) Since they can, in a sense, select relevant features of their environment, these systems might be used to replace the manager of Chapter 4, and hence have practical importance.

'change our reference frame' only means that we perform different conceptual experiments, try to make sense of unitary actions, sequences of actions and so on, in short, that we 'converse'. The rules of evolution and development are determined by the connectivity of an albeit very flexible computer, a network so constructed that the fabric form which it is made will be irrelevant. On the other hand, if we look at self-organizing systems in the real world, their evolution and development is determined by their fabric and because of this, 'changing our reference frame' comes to mean making physically different – often incomparable – kinds of experiment.

Auerbach's paper on the development of kidney tubules[82] illustrates the point. In the embryo the ureteric bud, which is the precursor of a duct connected to the tubules in the developed kidney, induces the mesenchymal cells to differentiate into a tubule, which is a readily recognized structure. Experimentally other tissues can be used to supply the *inducing* stimulus. After a group of cells have been in contact with an experimental inducing stimulus for 30 hours, the stimulus can be removed and the tubule structure which has, by then, appeared will persist and develop. We thus say that the control system 'kidney tubule' is 'tissue stable' for the organization that produces the visible structure is inherent in the tissue. However, at this stage, it is not inherent in the cell (as demonstrated by experiments involving disaggregation). But, 'cell stability', whereby cells have the property of differentiating into bits of tubules, *does* appear when the individual cells have been in contact with a stable tissue somewhat longer. Hence, the control system 'kidney tubule' entails at least two mechanisms which are not only 'different' but of a different *kind*, investigable by different sorts of inquiry, and if we had approached the matter without the benefit of this work, we should have suffered *structural* uncertainty about the *kind* of inquiry to make. However, a process of development would still have been manifest. The system would have seemed to us self-organizing. (I am using this work to make a point. The entire mechanism is still unknown and Auerbach calls the system 'self-organizing' even in the present state of knowledge.)

Development of an organism from a single germ cell into a multicellular entity is a self-organizing system from any point of view, and I wish to contend that *this* self-organizing system is a subsystem of the self-organizing system called 'evolution'. The statement is profound but, as I have put it, largely vacuous. It is made precisely (in biological rather than cybernetic terms) by J. T. Bonner who, for purposes of his discussion, adopts the view that it is 'development' that evolves rather than the 'organism' (his book, *The Evolution of Development*[83] is essential reading). Phrased differently, development takes place at all because of two competing evolutionary requirements. The first, the need to control the variability which comes from mutation, dictates a unicellular form. The control mechanism is commonly sex, though there are alternatives. The other requirement is for a large multicellular individual which is best fitted to survive in its environment. Evolution produces the mechanism called alternation of generations and the process of development from embryo to adult.

Notice, we have seen no alternation of generations in abstract evolutionary systems, though such an adaptation is conceivable and an alternative mechanism, of the kind Bonner describes for the slime molds, can be cited.[36] It is, after all, an adaptation to a particular fabric, protein, and a particular environment. The distinction between self-organization and life rests in fabric and it is significant because we, ourselves, are made from the same stuff as the things *we are prepared to call* 'alive'.

Abstract Approach

To complete the picture, there is Rashevsky's[20] view of evolution. The organism, regarded as a control system, can be mapped on to an image wherein all metrical properties are discarded, but all 'structural' relations preserved. The image will be a graph of the kind we used to depict states, only, in this case, the nodal points represent biological properties such as 'feeding' and 'secretion'. Rashevsky contends that the various graphs which have arisen by evolution can be transformed into one another – which is incontravertible if we accept the regularity of the real world – and are derivable from a primordial graph by repeated application, representing stages in evolution, of a single topological transformation T, some parameters of which are variable. For reasonable choice of T the primordial graph is a homomorph of any later graph and it is possible to 'work backwards'. Now T

is unknown but presumably it can be discovered by judicious comparison between the mathematical possibilities and the biological facts in order to obtain a 'best fit'.

Chemical Computers

In the energetic conditions of the real world protein is probably the only fabric which exhibits the stability and variety needed to maintain a self-organizing system. Life depends upon certain wavelengths of light being available for photosynthesis by plants. This energy can only be absorbed by a sub-set of possible macromolecules and only a limited number of these match the energy transfer systems of the required kind. But, given a different environment, other fabrics will sustain self-organizing systems, and I shall describe some artifacts made to illustrate the point which have, incidentally, a promising industrial application. They are chemical computers.

Chemical computers[84] arise from the possibility of 'growing' an active evolutionary network by an electro-chemical process. (D. M. MacKay has used the same process for producing 'analogue' connective elements in a computing machine.) Consider a very shallow perspex dish containing a moderately conductive acid solution of a metallic salt, an aqueous solution of ferrous sulphate, or an alcoholic solution of stannous chloride, with inert platinum wire electrodes α, β and X. If α is energized, a highly conductive dendrite or thread of metal will grow from X towards α, by electrodeposition. For each surface element, electrodeposition must keep pace with an acid back reaction, that is tending to dissolve the metal away, if the thread is to survive as a stable entity. Assuming stability, growth occurs as in Figure 22 (i).

Now, if we energize β, growth may occur towards α alone, β alone, or if there is enough total current, by bifurcation as in (ii). At this stage β is disconnected, but the subsequent growth of the thread is permanently modified because the branch y which is due to the intermediate energizing of β distorts the current distribution. Hence, we get (iii) instead of (iv) which would have appeared if β had not been energized. This is one sort of 'memory' which occurs because a dendrite grows in an electrical environment determined by itself and its neighbours. Another kind of memory is demonstrated in (v), (vi), (vii) and (viii), and amounts to reproduction. Assume the thread structure of (v) due to

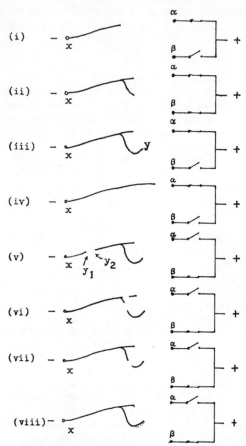

Fig. 22. Development of Thread Structures

previous manipulation of the energizing switch. Now this structure could not possibly be due to the β connection alone. Cut the thread at y_1/y_2 to form a gap. This gap, given current through β, moves up the thread, metal dissolving at y_1 and depositing at y_2. Almost complete regeneration is possible at (vi), (vii), (viii) which, simply because the thread structure is a large conductive surface, is substantially independent of the outside environment – in this case the setting of the energizing switch. We used these threads to grow connective networks between 'artificial neurones' which energized the electrodes in place of the switches. (Plate III (i) (ii) (iii) and (iv).) Since then we have concentrated upon 'instable threads'. The back reaction can be adjusted so that any thread is continually breaking and being regenerated. These instable threads perform the non-linear energy conversion of an artificial neurone and, to cut a long story short, we no longer require the 'artificial neurones' as such. Given some approximation to a distributed energy storage, which is difficult, but possible, a dish of solution on its own will give rise to the entire evolutionary network – connections and active devices. The first system of this kind was developed in collaboration with A. Addison at the University of Illinois, and Plate III (B) shows some of these threads in an experimental arrangement. Figure 23 is a tracing of the impulse output waveform from the arbitrarily placed sensory electrode shown in Plate III (A).

$\leftarrow \frac{1}{10}$ secs $\rightarrow$

Fig. 23

Using total energy inflow or, in the recent model, concentration of free metal ions as the reward variable θ it is possible to select those systems which have an acceptable electrical behaviour and reject others. But there is one trick you can play with this toy that is impossible with the networks we have already discussed. In those, there were components, with definite (even though primitive) functions assigned to them. Here there is only raw material – metal ions. Naturally we think of the raw material as stuff to make connection, but that is *our* hunch. Suppose we set up a device that rewards the system if, and only if, whenever a buzzer sounds, the buzzer frequency appears at the sensory electrode. Now a crazy machine like this is responsive to almost anything, vibration included (*components* are made to avoid such interference), so it is not surprising that occasionally the network does pick up the buzzer. The point is this. If picking it up is rewarded, the system gets better at the job and structures develop and replicate in the network which are specifically adapted as sound detectors. By definition, intent and design this cannot occur in an artifact made from well-specified components. It is an important property. When the active elements of a hill climber meet an insoluble problem, the uncertainty about which of several possible actions to take is resolved by a dice throw. The thread, faced with the same dilemma, must become one kind of thing or another – there is no finite set of *possibilities* to choose between – and from the observer's viewpoint a structural uncertainty is resolved. This is precisely the behaviour remarked upon by the earlier embroyologists – that development of a cell along a quantitative gradient gave rise to qualitative change.

The trick works with many variables. In a crude way this is a self-organizing system that can select those attributes of its environment which it must sense in order to survive. Of course, it is too crude to be useful. But improvements are coming. Bowman[85] recently proposed macromolecules acting as transmission lines, which would have the property in a manageable form, and George Zopf is actively pursuing the topic at the University of Illinois.

8 Industrial Cybernetics

THE chairman said '... our company is not its wealth, nor its factories, gentlemen, the old lot or the new 'uns' (he adjusted his tie), 'these' (he glared at the reading desk) 'are mere trappings. Our company's a living thing, gentlemen. It grows.' He sat down, flushed and wheezing. The executives clapped, excusing the diction of a self-made man. They reckoned him old fashioned, a bit poetic in his dotage. But, in fact, the self-made man had told a revolutionary truth, as he had told it before, badly, and without the faintest idea what to do about it. Had they listened, and understood, it would have shaken them to the bottom of their incentive schemes and order schedules.

Its Impact

Stafford Beer,[86, 87, 88, 89,] has stressed this essentially cybernetic concept; that industry is an organism; in a usefully expanded, cogent and decisive fashion. He means us to take the statement literally, not as an after-dinner analogy. A particular industry has the same trouble in preserving its identity and surviving amidst the flux of its environment as any animal. It either evolves or decays.

Having discussed the properties of organisms we know what to expect, and it will be more profitable to dwell upon the impact of Stafford Beer's idea. To the accountant, for example, it means that his model of the company, his precious double-entry stuff, is but a tiny facet of the truth. Something like an increase in profit is no measure for the health of an organism (he realized this before, of course, and thought it odd – but did not mention the matter). Nor is there any unique measure of growth, for it is the growth of an organism, and that upsets the assumption that an *optimum* condition *can* be achieved by some manipulation of sub-optima such as 'maximize turnover', 'maximize productivity' and others. To the operational research people it means that their models need rethinking. True, at a reflex level, simple feedbacks to simple operations, there is little change. But the organism, industry, has a vast redundancy of mechanism and the structural certainty has gone. To the manager it means that management cannot be efficient as well as authoritarian. It is an issue of persuasion, compromise and catalysis. He always knew that men and machines were cussed. Cybernetics offers a scientific approach to the cussedness of organisms, suggests how their behaviours can be catalysed and the mystique and rule of thumb banished.

What about the engineer? Just now there is plenty of conventional automation, but in a few years he will find this organism disconcerting. After all, engineers are accustomed to computers that sit in large, metal boxes, have sensory elements in a process and effectors that they control. Amongst the next batch of computers there will be some that are chunks of polymer, made to exist inside reaction vessels, and catalyse reactions with which they are in contact. The sensing and computing will not be distinct and maybe the effectors will also form part of the same thing.*

The Structure of Industry

We have argued the virtues of partitioning, hierarchical structure and division of labour sufficiently to take their existence for granted and only discuss how they should be brought about. Now, in an organism an hierarchy will not be described by an organization chart (at any rate, not of the currently drawn, inflexible kind, where A is responsible to B and C refers the matter to D, taking action if E sends a copy to F). From the recent literature it looks as though the men who draw these charts (and, heaven forbid, even put them into practice) would agree. They have reached the nasty-tasting conclusion that not every individual does fit into a niche. Indeed, an organization composed of individuals that do, is formally moribund. It is comforting to realize that the glorified, stratified, feudalized empires of industry work *because* the chart *is* disobeyed, that without the grace of local imperfection the whole structure would be instable as a house of

---

*A further possibility, amusing in its own way, is an animal computer, which could be valuable for slow speed, essentially parallel data processing. Skinner once used pretrained pigeons[90] as pattern recognizing automata in a guidance mechanism, and they have also been used in industry. Working along somewhat different lines Beer and I have experimented with responsive unicellulars as basic computing elements which are automatically reproducing and available in quantity.

cards (or a brain without its reticular formation). For stability by design rather than by default, the people who get things done must be allowed to run from niche to niche and communicate with their colleagues in real words, not duplicated advice notes. I will go even further and say, in an efficient biological hierarchy, each member must have the possibility, however small, of inverting the structure without leaving his niche to do so. I do not mean 'the office boy can rise to be manager'. I mean, 'in some unspecified conditions the office boy can take the managerial decisions' – when that would be a fitting adaptation.

Now it is easy to cite some kinds of process where my proposal is sheer nonsense. Mass production and routine data processing, for example, are most efficient when rigidly organized. Very well, then, have automata to do the stupid jobs that are entailed. A robot is more reliable than a man and, by definition of the work schedule, readily constructed. Any process best represented by a production chart can be *completely* automated. There are even robots for assembly jobs which used to be an exception to this rule.

The point was made most elegantly by Norbert Wiener[91] in *The Human Use of Human Beings*. Define 'man' functionally (the alternative, as a 'bag of chemicals', I find unacceptable), and he is at least an adaptive decision maker. To use him where neither choice nor adaptation are called for is not a human use. Conversely, automation never put a man (in this functional sense) out of work. If it does stop him playing the robot so much the better, for too much imitation makes us robot like. In particular, it is both distasteful and dangerous to regard man as a cheap substitute for an automaton – dangerous because there is a vicious circle and ultimately man will lose.

There still remains the question; who will pay the men who used to play at robots? Overall, two possibilities occur. First, the added efficiency of the process (demand for its product assumed) makes it possible to sustain these people in more human pursuits (there is some quantitative evidence in favour of this possibility). Otherwise rethink the concept of efficiency, and organize the process so that it is most efficient, *given the maximum utilization of human beings*. This, I agree, does not necessarily entail maximum short-term productivity, but I assume a certain social responsibility on the part of management.

Decision Making

Who or what can take managerial decisions? It is perfectly obvious that *managers* are unable to deal with the problems of modern industry. If you rig up a computer to give a manager all the information he needs about the state of the factory, it is necessary to include about a day's lag – otherwise he decides in a frenzy of misguided zeal that leaves the place in a shambles. He is not stupid. On the contrary, he is a highly trained, intelligent man. His decision capacity is simply overloaded. But, if you cannot tolerate the lag, and, nowadays, we cannot, the manager must be replaced.

An obvious solution lies in 'Two heads are better than one'. But, whilst true in a way, this adage was always defective. You cannot add wisdom by adding heads on a committee. That is the fallacy of team research (you cannot buy a research team. With luck it grows, making its own common language and thriving on personal interplay which has nothing to do with research). I suspect it is also fallacy of managerial groups.

How, then, can we combine the brains in the available heads? First, can we do it? Yes. There are existence proofs. Research teams that *do* work. Often enough husband and wife share a common language and make jointly wise decisions. I have seen the process also in groups of actors at club theatres, amongst jazz musicians and in football teams. These are stable communities that make genuine group decisions. Of course, they play at decision making all day long, and respond concertedly when a familiar situation appears in the real world. The *rapport* between horse and rider is not dissimilar; they decide together about the terrain. But, I have never seen this efficient organization in industry. The atmosphere is too earnest (maybe it must be). There is something that makes us approach the paper mill with a ponderous solemnity alien to a honky tonk. For all that, it may not be impossible to recapture some of the requisite abandon, by having managers play together via an adaptive machine. By analogy, the managers ride the same horse and the terrain is replaced by an image of their factory. At any rate, some serious work is in progress.

A second, closely related solution to the problem occurs when the industry is, in any case, biologically organized. Then there is redundancy of potential command. The whole system is interacting very closely indeed with the little microcosm of managers. Now, in this situation, we can never say where a decision is made, or that one bit of the whole melange is a control mechanism. The best we can do is to point out a badly distinguished managerial group and say that decisive activity is probably dense in this region.

Suppose that for some reason (size, speed, or elaboration) this knot of dense decision making cannot be a group of men but must be an evolutionary network. We have dwelt enough upon its possible form. Now look at the much more important question; given an evolutionary network, what would induce you to trust it as a decision maker? Not its cleverness, for it can be as clever as we can afford. I believe our confidence can only stem from our experience in conversation with it – and I propose two different tests. In the first, acting as a potential employee I should ask 'Can I owe allegiance to this network?', accepting it only if the answer is in the affirmative. Now, for my own part, I cannot owe allegiance to a box of tricks; to a programme – regardless of whether it is embodied in a computer or worked out in stereotype by a human board. This attitude 'allegiance' is a relation between persons, and the object of it must be an individual, or a group of people with its own personality. I think I should credit the network with this quality only in so far as it seemed to understand, even if it rejected, my contribution to the decisions in hand.

Next, acting as its potential employer, I should interview the network, taking its previous experience and behaviour into account. But, more important than this is the question of whether, in some sense, the network is like my image of myself being a manager (this part of the interview is difficult, for there is no verbal communication – but the essential requirement is that the network be capable of its own kind of discourse beyond the bounds of management). On this test, I shall accept the network if and only if it sometimes laughs outright. Which, in conclusion, is not impossible.

Glossary

ABDUCTION The process of arriving at a new kind of rule or logical model.

ADAPTIVE CONTROLLER A controller that can adapt (or modify) its control strategy (or programme of action).

ARTIFACT Devices constructed to simulate some aspect of behaviour.

ASSEMBLY A part of the real world selected for observation.

ATTRIBUTE An observable property of an assembly.

AUTOMATON (*see* ARTIFACT).

BINARY NUMBER A number, each figure of which can assume one of two values, 1 or 0.

BRAIN STEM A lower part of the brain – at the top of the spinal cord – which contains, amongst other things, the centres for respiratory and cardiac control.

CATALYST A material which accelerates one or a few out of many possible reactions. An autocatalyst is a catalyst produced as a product of the reaction it catalyses. The word comes from chemistry, but is used in cybernetics in connexion with all kinds of change in the state of systems.

CELL The building block from which organisms are constructed.

CHANNEL That part of a communication system along which messages are conveyed, or its mathematical representation.

CODE A rearrangement of the signals that convey a message.

CEREBRAL CORTEX A relatively undifferentiated higher region of the brain.

DEDUCTION The process of working out the consequences of a given set of rules, or of a logical model.

ENZYME A biological catalyst.

EQUILIBRIUM A state of a system which keep certain properties invariant. The term includes not only static equilibria – an object at rest – but also dynamic equilibria and statistical equilibria.

EVOLUTION Either the process observed in nature, or a comparable process occurring in an artifact.

FEEDBACK Return of a signal, indicating the result of an action, in order to determine further actions.

GENE A unit (in fact, a collection of 'nucleic acids') which conveys the hereditary information for building an organism (the genes are arranged on chromosomes in the nucleus of each cell).

114

GESTALT Some property – such as roundness – common to a set of sense data and appreciated by organisms or artifacts.

HOMEOSTASIS The regulation of variables important to the survival or well being of an organism.

HORMONE A specific chemical released by specialised tissues in an organism, the presence of which acts as a signal to other tissues.

INDUCTION Making inferences from given evidence, for example, the evidence provided by experimental observations.

INFORMATION A measure of selection amongst a given set of possibilities. Sometimes a measure of the extent to which uncertainty is reduced.

MATRIX An array of numbers used, in mathematics, to specify the transformation of a vector.

METALANGUAGE A descriptive language such as the language in which an observer describes a discussion between two participants that takes place in an 'object language'.

NEURONE A cell in the central nervous system with the specialized function of signalling. An artificial neurone is a device which simulates a few of the characteristics of a real neurone.

NUCLEUS A dense region in the cell concerned, amongst other things, with the control of protein synthesis and reproduction.

PROBABILITY A numerical measure of certainty with various technical usages.

RETINA An array of light receptors, either in the eye of an animal or forming part of an artifact.

REFERENCE FRAME A collection of comparable systems.

SET, SUB-SET Any collection of objects or entities.

SERVOMECHANISM A mechanical device using negative feedback and often maintaining a predetermined or remotely adjusted motion or position.

STABILITY A condition in which a system is controllable.

STATE A recognizable condition of a system.

STATIONARY SYSTEM A system which is in dynamic or statistical equilibrium. Its statistical characteristics do not change. In a non-stationary system the statistical characteristics do change.

SYNAPSE The organized junction between neurones.

SYSTEM Roughly, a collection of states together with the rules whereby they change, but it is a technical term.

TAUTOLOGOUS ARGUMENT is circular

TELEOLOGICAL ARGUMENT entails the idea of purpose

TRANSFORMATION A mathematical expression of change.

ULTRASTABILITY The form of stability apparent in an adaptive system, in particular, an adaptive controller.

VARIABLE The changeable quantity that appears in a mathematical relation. Attributes of an assembly are identified with the variables in a mathematical model to form a system.

VARIATION Production of novel forms or structures, in natural evolution the production of mutants.

VARIETY A measure of uncertainty or the amount of selection needed to remove the uncertainty.

VECTOR An ordered set of numbers that specify the values of variables.

References

A. *Mechanization of Thought Processes*, N.P.L. Symposium 10, H.M. Stationery Office, 1959.

B. *Self-Organizing Systems*, O.N.R. and Armour Foundation Symposium, Ed. Marshall Yovits and Scott Cameron, Pergamon Press, 1960.

C. *Automata Studies*, Ed. C. E. Shannon and J. McCarthey, No. 34, Princeton Univ. Press, 1956.

D. Proc. 2nd Congress International Association of Cybernetics, Namur, 1958. Gauthier Villars (in press).

E. Proc. 1st Congress International Association of Cybernetics, Namur, 1956. Gauthier Villars, 1959.

F. Proc. 4th London Symposium on Information Theory (to be published soon).

G. Urbana Symposium on the Principles of Self Organization, 1960, to be published by Pergamon Press.

H. Brookhaven Symposium in Biology, 10, 'Homeostatic Mechanisms, '1957.

I. Proc. 1st London Symposium on Information Theory, 1950.

1. Boulanger, G. R., *Presidential Address*, D.

2. Cannon, W. B., *Wisdom of the Body*, London, 1932.

3. Goldman, Stanford, *Cybernetic Aspects of Homeostasis*, B.

4. Benzinger, T. H., *Human Thermostat*, Scientific American, Jan. 1961.

5. Peterson, E. W.; Magoun, H. W.; Lindsley, D. B.; McCulloch, W. S.; *Production of Postural Tremor*, J. Neurophysiology, 12, 1949.

6. Weiss, Paul, *Animal Behaviour as a System Reaction*. Reprinted in *General Systems Yearbook*, Vol. 4, 1959.

7. Von Bertalanffy, Ludwig, *General System Theory*. Reprinted in *General Systems Yearbook*, Vol. 1, 1956.

8. Weiner, Norbert, *Cybernetics*, Technology Press and John Wiley, 1948.

9. Rosenblueth, A.; Weiner, N.; Bigelow, J., *Behaviour Purpose and Teleology*, Philosophy of Science, 10, Baltimore, 1943.

10. Couffignal, Louis, *Essai d'une definition generale de la Cybernetique*, D.

11. Beer, Stafford, *Cybernetics and Management*, English Universities Press, 1960.

12. Ashby, Ross, *Introduction to Cybernetics*, Chapman and Hall, 1956.

13. Pask, Gordon, *Organic Control and the Cybernetic Method*, Cybernetica, IV, 1958.

14. Buck, R. C., *On the Logic of General Behaviour Systems Theory*, Minnesota Studies in Philosophy of Science, Vol. 1, 1956, Minnesota Press.

15. Deutsch, J. A., *A Machine with Insight*, Qutly. Jnl. of Experimental Psychology, Vol. VI, Part 1, 1954.

16. Ashby, Ross, *Design for a Brain*, Chapman and Hall, 2nd Ed., 1960.

17. Braithwaite, R. B., *Scientific Explanation*, Cambridge Univ. Press, 1952.

18. MacKay, D. M., *Quantal Aspects of Scientific Information*, Phil Mag., 1950, 41, also in I.

19. Coombs, B.; Raiffa, C. H.; and Thrall, R. M., *Some Views on Mathematical Models*, 'Decision Processes', John Wiley and Sons, and Chapman and Hall, 1952.

20. Rashevsky, N., *Mathematical Biophysics*, Dover, 1960.

21. Pask, Gordon, *Physical Analogues to the Growth of a Concept*, A.

22. Nagel, E., *The Meaning of Reduction in the Natural Sciences*, Sciences and Civilization, edited R. C. Stauffer, Univ. of Wisconsin Press, 1949.

23. Cherry, Colin, *On Human Communication*, Technology Press and John Wiley, 1957.

24. Popper, K. R., *The Logic of Scientific Discovery*, Hutchinson, 1959.

25. Rapoport, A., and Rebhun, L., Bull. Math. Biophysics, 14, 1952. Also Rapoport, A., Bul. Math. Biophysics, 15, 1953, and 16, 1954.

26. Turing, A. M., *On Computable Numbers with an Application to the Entscheisdungsproblem*, Proc. London Math. Soc. 2, 42, 1937.

27. Von Foerster, H., *Biological Aspects of Homeostasis*, H.

28. Shannon, C. E., and Weaver, W., *The Mathematical Theory of Communication*, Univ of Illinois Press, 1949.

29. Kemeny, J. G., and Snell, J. L., *Finite Markoff Chains*, Van Nostrand, 1960.

30. Harlow, H. F., *Learning Set and Error Factor Theory*, Psychology; A Study of a Science, edited S. Koch. Vol. 2, 1959, McGraw Hill.

31. MacKay, D. M., *The Informational Analysis of Questions and Commands*, F.

32. Beer, Stafford, *Towards the Cybernetic Factory*, G.

33. Pringle, J. W. S., *On the Parallel between Learning and Evolution*, General Systems Yearbook, Vol. 1, 1956.

34. Von Foerster, H., *Environments of Self Organizing Systems*, B.

35. Pask, Gordon, *Natural History of Networks*, B.

36. Pask, Gordon, *A Proposed Evolutionary Model*, G.

37. MacColl, L. A., *Servomechanisms*, Van Nostrand, 1945.

38. Tustin, A., *The Mechanism of Economic Systems*, Harvard Univ. Press, 1953.

39. Ashby, Ross, *Design for an Intelligence Amplifier*, C.

40. Uttley, A. M., *Conditional Probability Machines and Conditioned Reflexes*, C.

41. Uttley, A. M., *Patterns in a Conditional Probability Machine*, C.

42. MacKay, D. M., *Epistemological Problem for Automata*, C.

43. Box, G. E., *Evolutionary Operation*, Applied Statistics, 4, 1957.

44. Andrew, A. M., *Learning Machines*, A.

45. George, F., *Probabilistic Machines*, Automation Progress, Vol. 3, No. 1.

46. Gabor, D., *A Universal Non Linear Predictor and Simulator which Optimizes itself by a Learning Process*, Proc. Inst. Electrical Engineers, 108, 1961.

47. Ivahnenko, A. G., Мехническа Кибернегика, Кцев, 1959.

48. McCulloch, W. S., *Agatha Tyche*, A.

49. McCulloch, W. S., *The Stability of Biological Systems*, H.

50. Stanley Jones, D. and K., *The Kybernetics of Natural Systems*, Pergamon Press, 1960.

51. *Information Theory in Biology*, edited H. Quastler, Univ. of Illinois Press, 1953.

52. Walter, Grey, *The Living Brain*, Duckworth, 1953.

53. Angyan, A. J., Kretz H., and Zemanek, H., *A Model for Neurophysiological Functions*, F.

54. Scholl, D. A., *The Organization of the Cerebral Cortex*, Methuen, 1956.

55. Lashley, K. S., *In Search of the Engram*, Symposia of the Society for Experimental Biology. *Physiological Mechanisms in Anima Behaviour*, Cambridge Univ. Press, 1950.

56. Eccles, J. C., *Neurophysiological Basis of Mind*, Oxford Univ. Press, 1953.

57. Beurle, R. L., *Properties of a Mass of Cells Capable of Regenerating Impulses*, Phil. Trans. Royal Society, 240, 1956.

58. Beurle, R. L., *Storage and Manipulation of Information in the Brain*, 5, New series, Jnl. of Inst. of Elec. Engs., 1959.

59. Crane, H. D., *Neuristor Studies*, Technical Report 1506, 2, Stanford Electronics Laboratories, 1960.

60. Foulkes, J. D., *A Class of Machine which determine the Statistica Structure of a Sequence of Inputs*, Western Electronics Show & Convention, San Francisco, 1959.

61. Farley, G. B., and Clark, W. A., *Activity in Network of Neuronelike Elements*, F.

62. Willis, G. D., *Plastic Neurones as Memory Elements*, Lockheed Report, LMSD 48432, 1959.

63. Babcock, Murray, *Reorganization by Adaptive Automaton*, Technical Report 1. Contract NONR 1834 (21), Elec. Eng. Research Labs., Univ. of Illinois.

64. Selfridge, O., and Minsky M., *Learning in Random Nets*, F.

65. Green, P., *An Approach to Computers that Perceive, Learn, and Reason*, Proc. Western Joint Computer Conf. 1959.

66. Von Foerster, H., and Pask, G., *A Predictive Model for Self Organizing Systems*, Cybernetica 4, 1960, and 1, 1961.

67. Newell, A.; Shaw, J. C.; and Simon, H. A., *A Variety of Intelligent Learning in a General Problem Solver*, B.

68. Cowan, Jack, *Many Valued Logics and Homeostatic Mechanisms* to be published in *Information and Control*.

69. Pitts, W., and McCulloch, W. S., *How We Know Universals, The Perception of Auditory and Visual Forms*, Bul. of Math. Biophysics, 9, 1947.

70. Pitts, W., and McCulloch, W. S., *Logical Calculus of Ideas Immanent in Nervous Activity*, Bul. of Math. Biophysics, 5, 1943.

71. Lettvin, J. Y.; Matturana, H. R.; McCulloch, W. S.,; and Pitts, W., *What the Frog's Eye Tells the Frog's Brain*, Proc. I.R.E., November, 1959.

72. Abercrombie, M. L. Johnson, *The Anatomy of Judgement*, Hutchinson, 1960.

73. Babcock, M. L.; Inselberg, A.; Lofgren, L.; Von Foerster, H.; Weston, P.; and Zopf, G. W., *Some Principles of Preorganization in Self-Organizing Systems*, Technical Report 2, Contract NONR 1834 (21), Elec. Eng. Research Labs., Univ. of Illinois, 1960.

74. Rosenblatt, F., *The Perceptron*, Cornell Aeronautical Lab. Report VG1196, 1, 1958, and subsequent reports. Also, *Two Theorems of Statistical Seperability, in the Perceptron*, A.

75. Selfridge, O., *Pandemonium, A Paradigm of Learning*, A.

76. *Teaching Machines and Programmed Learning*, edited by A. A. Lumsdaine and R. Glaser, is a volume which includes the source papers and full references in this field.

77. Pask, G., *The Teaching Machine as a Control Mechanism*, Trans. Society Instrument Technology, 12.2.1960.

78. Woodworth, R. S., *Experimental Psychology*, Methuen, 1951.

79. Lofgren, L., *Automata of High Complexity and Methods of Increasing their Reliability by Redundancy*, E.

80. Burks, A. W., *Computation, Behaviour and Structure*, B.

81. Penrose, P., *Self Reproducing Machine*, Scientific American, June, 1959.

82. Auerbach, R., *The Organization and Reorganization of Embryonic Cells*, B.

83. Bonner, J. T., *The Evolution of Development*, Cambridge Univ. Press, 1958.

84. Technical Reports of Contract NONR 1834(21), Elec. Eng. Research Labs., Univ. of Illinois. Also 18 and 32.

85. Bowman, J., Paper read at Urbana Symposium, G.

86. Beer, Stafford, *The Irrelevance of Automation*, D.

87. Beer, Stafford, *The Impact of Cybernetics on the Concept of Industrial Organization*, E.

88. Beer, Stafford, *Operational Research and Cybernetics*, E.

89. Beer, Stafford, *Overall Control in a New Context*, Inst. of Production Engineers.

90. Skinner, B. F., *Pigeons in a Pelican*, American Psychologist, 16, 1, 1960.

91. Wiener, N., *The Human Use of Human Beings*, Eyre and Spottiswoode, 2nd ed., 1955.

Appendix I

Distinction between structural and metrical aspects of information
(*see* Chapter 2, page 20)
The distinction between the structural and metrical aspects of
information was first made by Gabor and generalized by MacKay (18),
who developed a comprehensive theory of scientific information on
this basis. We are using the terms 'structural' and 'metrical' less precisely than MacKay (but in a closely related fashion) in order to demark the qualitative and quantitative content of a statement about
the world. Take a statement 'The boiler pressure is 100 lb. lb./sq. in.
to the nearest unit'. It has, for its qualitative (or structural) content, a
summary of what kind of result we should expect, namely one of the
possible Readings on a pressure gauge. We are not measuring a volume
or a surface tension. Nor can we expect indefinitely accurate evaluation
of pressure. The quantitative or metrical part of the statement says what
the result of the measurement actually is, namely 100 lb./sq. in. More
generally, 'structural information' specifies the events which may occur,
'metrical information' those events in this set which do occur. But at
this level some caution is needed.

   (i) There is a definite limitation to the smallness and specificity of
events which can be measured in a given interval Δt (the limitation
takes the form of an uncertainty principle. We avoid explicit discussion of this principle by stating the initial axiom, and assuming that
separate observations are spaced apart at least Δt).

   (ii) Given a set of events, different orders of measurement are
possible (corresponding to the mathematical model in which the
events are identified) (19). It is always possible to *name* the events. If
there are *neighbourhood* relations between elements in the event set
the set forms a *space* in which these elements are points. There may
or may not be a measure on this space, i.e. a numerically expressed
distance between the points.

Appendix 2

Choice of reference frames (*see* Chapter 2, page 23)
Although the reference frame depends upon the observer, his choice
is conditioned by all his previous experience and by convention. We
have, in science, rather stereotyped ways of looking at the world, and
the advantage of adopting them whenever possible has already been
pointed out – the measurements are comparable – and the systems
built up in the reference frame are communicable. A reference frame

such as the hypothetico deductive framework of physics also has a highly structured U and the results of confirming or denying an hypothesis are maximally informative. The reference frames of biology are less so, of psychology less still (consider the status of Tolman's intervening variable equations) and observations are correspondingly less informative. Further, in the behavioural sciences not all measurements are comparable. Nor are all systems (at the present state of knowledge we cannot strictly compare a Pavlovian system, a Hullian and a Hebbian system, not to mention the systems of psycho-analysis, though we may become able to compare them if a unifying theory is developed. As Nagel (22) points out, the construction of a translation language commonly entails theoretical *and* empirical advancement. The simplest form of empirical discovery is a *correlation* between events discerned in two previously incomparable reference frames). Finally, the reference frame of the cloud shadows world is less structured than any of these. The observer cannot help it for cloud shadows are not so well behaved as springs and spheres. They dissolve and reappear, whilst they are in motion, and the ideas of continuity, embedded in an elaborately structured U would lead to a manifestly implausible hypothesis. This observer is looking at a very black box. If he could see the clouds rather than their shadows, he would be better off, though clouds are bad enough.

Appendix 3

Transition probability matrix (*see* Chapter 3, page 43)
P is an *n.n.* matrix with n^2 entries p_{ij} and $\Sigma_i p_{ij} = 1$ rows and columns corresponding with the states. $J(t)$ is a column vector. Each row in the matrix represents the probability distribution obtained by selecting the state in correspondence with this row, as we do in multiplication with the column vector $J(t)$. The state of a Markovian system can be represented as a point in a probability space with n co-ordinates $p_1, p_2, \ldots p^n$ one to each state. This space should not be confused with the phase space with m co-ordinates related to the attributes.

Appendix 4

Ergodic Systems (*see* Chapter 3, page 45)
Four basic kinds of statistical equilibria are possible depending upon the behaviour of the powers of P.

(i) If the powers of P cease to change as r is increased so that $P^r = P^{r+1}$ the probability distribution becomes invariant, that is, $p_i(r) = p_i(r+1) = p^*$. Thus the state of the Markovian system is invariant and it can be shown that the values in the distribution p^* are independent of the initial state i. But any *representative system* can move from any state to any other state. In the phase space the state points of the ensemble are in continual motion, because a *representative* *system* can always reach any of the states (none of the transitions are impossible), the average population, at any instant, being determined by p^*. The equilibrium is called *ergodic* and the set of states which can be visited (in this case all the states) is called an *ergodic set*. Further the system is called *regular*, for each of the possible transitions can take place at any instant. A case of special importance occurs when $p^* = \frac{1}{n}, \frac{1}{n}, \cdots \frac{1}{n}$ and the state points of the representative systems are evenly distributed in the phase space.

(ii) If the powers of P form a cycle so that $P^r \neq P^{r+1}$, but $P^r = P^{r+u}$ for $n > u$ the equilibrium is *ergodic* and cyclic. In this case there are some 0 entries in P^r which move around as r is increased. Hence, a representative system can reach any state, but maybe only in several moves.

(iii) Other than ergodic, states are called transient states. If these exist there may be several different equilibrial ergodic sets. A transient state must eventually be vacated so the state of the system will eventually be one of the ergodic sets, but its probability of ending up in a particular one does now depend upon the initial state.

(iv) One or more ergodic sets include only one state, aptly dubbed a 'trapping state', for according to the argument cited above, any representative system must end up in a single 'trapping' state.

There is a further discussion of statistical equilibria in a paper by Von Foerster [27].

Appendix 5

Information Theory (*see* Chapter 3, page 45)
It is convenient to think about the behaviour of organisms and automata in terms of communication and computation and Information Theory. Let us briefly review some pertinent aspects of this field.

The Different Information Theories
There is still a significant difference between two groups of information theorists. Following Shannon and Weaver, information is a quantity, a number of yes - or - no decisions, called bits, sufficient to select one message from an ensemble of messages in a predetermined code ; whereas, following Gabor and MacKay, a quantity of scientific information has two aspects. The first, or logon content, is determined by the question asked and the second, or metron content, measures the assurance, and so determines the possible precision of measurements. The scientific information is given by Shannon's measure when there is but one metron per logon; that is, when the ensemble is not that of science in general but of an established code.

A Technical Usage of the Word 'Meaning'
Any event that can be detected by an organism or a machine may exercise some selective function upon the ensemble of transition probabilities of the behaviour of the detector (it operates upon the

statistical parameters of the system representing the detector). This function is, in Mackay's (31) words, its meaning.

There is a particular case we shall use later. Suppose the behaviour of a human being when he adopts one attitude is determined by a transition probability matrix P_1, when he adopts another by a transition probability matrix P_2, and that a set P of descriptive matrices encompass a sensible part of his behaviour. Now, to say the stochastic system representing a man *can* be described in this way also says it is partitionable. Hence we consider a selective operation F^* (as in the discussion of Chapter 3). Now F^* may be externally controlled by some system to which the man is coupled – say, for example, an instructor – and in this case certain messages from the instructor which lead the man to change his attitude induce a selection upon the ensemble P. By definition, the meaning of such a message is its selective function, with respect to P. Notice, the meaning entails the *relation* between the message source and the recipient.

Shannon's Statistical Information Theory

The basic model for statistical information theory involves a source, channel and receiver. When dealing with such tenuously specified objects as organisms it is particularly important to avoid facile analogy and keep within the limitations of a rigid model. The statistical measure applies *only* to this model; it is computed by an *outside* observer (*not*, for example, by the organism even if the organism is itself another observer) and the model is defined in his metalanguage. Information is a quantity of selection. The nature of the entities selected, like the issue of 'meaning', does not enter into the theory.

The source is an ergodic process with n states. State transitions select symbols (letters, words, dots and dashes) from a well-defined alphabet for transmission along the channel.

First, assume independence of selections. If the receiver is aware of transition probabilities p_i, $i = 1, 2, \ldots n$ (and ergodicity guarantees ζ_i that converge to p_i) the information which can be *delivered* by the source will be

$$V = - \sum_i p_i \cdot \text{Log}_2 \, p_i \text{ per } \Delta t \text{ or per selection.}$$

V is also a measure of the amount the receiver's uncertainty about the source is *reduced* by reception of messages. If the states are equally likely to occur $p_i = \dfrac{1}{n}$ and $V = -\text{Log}_2.n$ which is its maximal value. If, on the other hand, the receiver has knowledge of sequential dependencies the information which can be delivered is reduced. Taking two stage dependencies alone

$$V^* = - \sum_i \sum_j p_i \cdot p_{ij} \cdot \text{Log}_2 \, p^i \quad :$$

where the $j = 1, 2, \ldots n$.

The messages from such a source are called 'redundant' (and the ratio $1 - \dfrac{V^*}{V_{max}}$ where V_{max} is the maximum information the source could deliver is called the redundancy). Due to its statistical knowledge the receiver may deem certain messages 'inconceivable' and, within limits, can compensate for imperfections which exist in any real channel and distort any real message.

Take written language, for example, where we automatically regard the word 'commuxications' as a misprint of the word 'communications'. The original message has been distorted in the channel of the printed page but because the receiver is aware that the probability of 'x' after 'u' is low and of 'n' after 'u' is rather high the distortion can be plausibly rectified.

Ideally, a communication channel should effect a one to one transformation of messages. Distortion implies a many valued transformation and can be represented as the introduction of *irrelevant* signals or 'noise' which render a *relevant* message – i.e. one from the source – ambiguous. If the 'noise' is not wholly unrestricted its effect can be minimized by suitable coding schemes.

Different Forms of Signal

We commonly divide signals, somewhat arbitrarily, into those which are continuous, like the sound of speech or its electrical transform in telephony, or the concentration of a specific chemical 'hormone' in the bloodstream, and those that are discrete, like the dots and dashes of Morse telegraphy or the pips of radar. A precise transform of a continuous signal requires instruments equally precise and consequently expensive; and no combination of them permits us to compute the value of a variable beyond the precision of the least precise component. Our only hope of accuracy lies in the repititious nature of the messages themselves. Discrete signals carry with them greater assurance, for the instrument only needs to decide which one of a few signals occurred. The indifference to the exact size of the signal may replace repetition of the signal, for the value of its amplitude can be ignored except for the decision of whether or not it is less or greater than a single value, the threshold of the component. If it trips a relay we may combine it with others to compute as precisely as we will, and the components need only be good enough to make the decision, and are, consequently, cheap. Nature employs them in brains and man in his digital computers. Generally the discrete signals leave less uncertainty about their source than continuous signals both for organisms and for machines. Various coding schemes, more or less efficient, more or less fallible can be used; for example, in a discrete system the intervals between individual pips may or may not be a signal and able to convey information. Brains, like machines, appear to use several schemes in organizing their behaviour.

Appendix 6

A Markovian System (see Chapter 3, page 46)

A system which is Markovian when observed in n states may not be Markovian if the observer combines some of his states and inspects a less detailed image. Let D_i, D_j, be any combined states, for example, let $D_i = (1, 2)$ and $D_j = (3, 4)$ where $1, 2, ..k..n$, are states of the original Markovian system with transition matrix P. Now P is said to be 'lumpable' [29] with respect to the chosen combinations of states, if pkD_i [18] is the same for each original state k in D_j. If P is lumpable the less detailed 'lumped' system P^* is also a Markovian system (this is analogous to the homomorph of a state determined system which is always another state determined system). Expansion of a Markovian system to take account of sequential dependencies is reversed by lumping.

Appendix 7

The Neuristor (*see* Chapter 5, page 80)

Crane has recently worked out the logical possibilities of an active transmission line, wherein an impulse is transmitted at the cost of locally stored energy. When energy is dissipated it gives rise to a sensitizing wave that alters a non-linear characteristic of an adjacent element of the constructional medium leading to further local dissipation. It is called the 'Neuristor', since a nerve fibre is a special case realized in an aqueous medium. He shows that all Boolean and probabilistic functions can be computed using 'neuristor' circuits. If the elements in Beurle's network are indefinitely reduced they become, with suitable choice of parameters, elements in a neuristor network.

Index

127